Oxford Advanced Learner's Dictionary

Resource Book

OXFORD

UNIVERSITY PRESS

OXFORD
UNIVERSITY PRESS

Great Clarendon Street, Oxford OX2 6DP

Oxford University Press is a department of the University of Oxford.
It furthers the University's objective of excellence in research, scholarship,
and education by publishing worldwide in

Oxford New York

Auckland Cape Town Dar es Salaam Hong Kong Karachi
Kuala Lumpur Madrid Melbourne Mexico City Nairobi
New Delhi Shanghai Taipei Toronto

With offices in

Argentina Austria Brazil Chile Czech Republic France Greece
Guatemala Hungary Italy Japan Poland Portugal Singapore
South Korea Switzerland Thailand Turkey Ukraine Vietnam

OXFORD and OXFORD ENGLISH are registered trade marks of
Oxford University Press in the UK and in certain other countries

ISBN-13: 978 0 19 431699 6
ISBN-10: 0 19 431699 8

Printed in China

ACKNOWLEDGEMENTS

Text: Jennifer Bradbery, Victoria Bull, Margaret Deuter,
Diana Lea, Joseph Noble, Johanna Stirling

We would like to thank the following for their permission to reproduce photographs:
Hemera Technologies Inc.

Illustrations: Marta Cone, David Eaton, Elizabeth Gaus,
Matthew Hansen, Margaret Jones, Martin Lonsdale,
Mike Malkovas, Martin Shovel, Susan Van Winkle

Design: Pauline Hall, P Squared Design

Cover design: Philip Hargraves

Introduction

Dictionary skills training in the classroom

These exercises and activities are designed to help students make fuller and more effective use of the *Oxford Advanced Learner's Dictionary* seventh edition. They are a lively and enjoyable way to develop students' dictionary skills and at the same time expand the range and depth of their vocabulary.

The seventh edition of *OALD*, as a source of information about English for learners, is unrivalled in its breadth of coverage and in the help it gives students. But to benefit fully from this resource, students need to be able to access that information quickly and efficiently. As learners are often unaware of dictionary conventions, training in using them is particularly important. This book provides the basis for such training.

The exercise and activity pages are photocopiable and easy to use in the classroom as a means of introducing dictionary work at upper intermediate and advanced levels. In addition, most of the exercises can be done by students working on their own. Teachers will find useful advice on presenting the exercises at the back of the book.

Integrating dictionary use into lessons

The exercises and activities in this book focus specifically on dictionary use, but the dictionary should become an integral part of every lesson, including those which focus on other parts of the syllabus, such as the traditional four skills of reading, writing, listening and speaking.

One of the key principles in using dictionaries to learn vocabulary is that the more mental processing takes place regarding a particular vocabulary item, the more likely it is to be retained in the memory. In general, it is far preferable for students to find the information from the dictionary themselves rather than have it provided by the teacher. So, for example, when students are working on a text in groups, negotiation of which words to look up and discussion of the findings will help the words to 'stick'.

Another useful approach is to pre-teach vocabulary by dictating a list of words which are likely to be new to students and which they are about to

encounter in a text. Students must convert the phonological information received into plausible spellings, again by means of negotiation and discussion, and then locate the vocabulary items in their dictionaries.

A useful technique for intermediate students who may not know all of the items on the *Oxford 3000*™ keyword list (see section 19) would be to differentiate the words in a text which are part of the list from those which are not, perhaps by underlining them in different colours.

Teachers should not worry if students do not remember everything that they look up. Words can easily be looked up again, and each repetition will reinforce that word in the memory.

Using dictionaries for independent learning

Unfamiliar vocabulary presents a challenge for all learners. Good training will encourage students to be selective in the words they look up, and to choose words that occur frequently in a text, or which seem to be important for an understanding of it. When reading independently for pleasure or study, students may find it discouraging to have to look up a high proportion of vocabulary items, especially when most may be either incidental to the overall meaning or easily inferable.

Students should be encouraged to attempt to infer meaning from the form of a word and its context (this will form part of the mental processing mentioned above) before turning to the dictionary. Students may be less willing to look up words they think they know, but which are used in a wide variety of different ways that they may not be aware of. Knowledge of the different aspects that make up a word (meaning, pronunciation, context, etc.) is actually more important than knowing a large number of words. Close study of the *Oxford 3000* is an ideal way to increase the depth of their vocabulary knowledge.

The more often students use their dictionary, the more use they will find for it. It is hoped that this *Resource Book* will be a stimulus to embark on a surprising and rewarding journey of discovery, which will continue long after the end of the English lesson.

Contents

1 Finding your way around the dictionary

A Alphabetical order

1.1 Put these words into alphabetical order.

■ **a**

wheat	_____
rye	_____
barley	___1___
millet	_____
oats	_____
maize	_____
corn	_____
rice	_____

■ **b**

pipette	_____
pitch	_____
piquant	_____
pipeline	_____
pith	_____
pipe organ	_____
pit stop	_____
pistachio	_____

■ **c**

seep	_____
seize	_____
segment	_____
select	_____
seizure	_____
seismic	_____
sieve	_____
siesta	_____

■ **d**

ski pants	_____
skid	_____
skinny	_____
skiing	_____
skier	_____
ski	_____
skin diving	_____
ski lift	_____

■ **e**

o'clock	_____
O-Bon	_____
O level	_____
OAP	_____
O	_____
o'	_____
OD	_____
odd	_____

B Finding the right page

1.2 Which of these words would you find on the pages that start with **seaside** and end with **second best**?

season	___✓___	segment	_____	second	_____
secondary school	_____	secluded	_____	secondary	_____
seat	_____	seclusion	_____		

1.3 Which of these words would you find on the pages that start with **me-too** and end with **Midas touch**?

mica	___✓___	middle age	_____	metre	_____
midday	_____	micron	_____	midfield	_____
metronome	_____	mews	_____	mighty	_____
midnight	_____				

C Finding the right part of speech

1.4 Look at these entries and write down what parts of speech these words can be.

bridge	_____
green	_____
extra	_____
fool	_____
prior	_____
so	_____

1.5 In which part of the entry (in other words, under which part of speech) would you look to find the meanings of the words in **bold** in these sentences?

1 It has been an exceptionally **dry** summer. _adjective_

2 It takes several hours for the paint to **dry**. _____

3 The countryside around is very **flat**. _____

4 They're moving to a new **flat**. _____

5 How long has she been **ill**? _____

6 They tend to blame drugs for all the **ills** of society. _____

7 He **motioned** to us to sit down. _____

8 Do not stand up when the bus is in **motion**. _____

9 I hope they'll get here **before** it gets dark. _____

10 Have you seen this film **before**? _____

D Homonyms

1.6 Study the entries for the words in the box and decide where the words in the sentences would fit.

1 The musicians took a **bow**. _bow¹_

2 The violinist raised his **bow**. _____

3 She tied the ribbon in a **bow**. _____

4 He had a **row** with his father. _____

5 Can you see that **row** of trees? _____

6 They decided to **row** across the lake. _____

7 The **lead** in my pencil's broken. _____

8 Where does this road **lead**? _____

9 France took an early **lead**. _____

10 Wait a **minute**! I'm nearly ready. _____

11 They found **minute** particles of dust in the air. _____

12 There were **tears** in her eyes. _____

13 Be careful you don't **tear** your trousers on those bushes. _____

14 Strong **winds** and heavy rain are forecast for all areas. _____

15 The road **winds** its way up the mountain. _____

> bow¹ /baʊ/; bow² /bəʊ, boʊ/
> row¹ /rəʊ, roʊ/; row² /raʊ/
> lead¹ /liːd/; lead² /led/
> minute¹ /ˈmɪnɪt/; minute² /maɪˈnjuːt/
> tear¹ /teə(r), ter/; tear² /tɪə(r), tɪr/
> wind¹ /wɪnd/; wind² /waɪnd/

E Inflected forms

1.7 Write down the headword where you would look to find these words.

jetties	_jetty_	fretting	_____
intensifies	_____	bumpier	_____
cruellest	_____	frolicked	_____
grabbed	_____	fatter	_____

➜ If an irregular form is very different from its base form, and comes at a different place in the alphabet, you will find a cross-reference there.

F Choosing the right meaning

1.8 Answer these questions:

1 How many meanings are given for the noun **lodge**?

2 Which of them is connected with animals?

3 How many meanings are given for the noun **lobby**?

4 Do any of them refer to people?

5 How many meanings can you find for the verb **drill**?

6 Which of them is to do with making holes?

7 For the verb **dribble**, three meanings are to do with liquids. In what context is the fourth meaning used?

8 The adjective **rambling** can be used to describe buildings. In what two other contexts is it used?

G Specialist fields

1.9 Look at the entries and note down in what specialist field they are used.

1	shelf	_geology_	5	bull	_____
2	maintenance	_____	6	attract	_____
3	benign	_____	7	basket	_____
4	backup	_____	8	article	_____

H Short cuts

1.10 Look at the entries for the words in **bold** in these sentences and write down the short cut under which you would find the appropriate meaning.

1 She was a famous **model**. _fashion_

2 What is the **scale** of this map? _____

3 He's a **mean** cook – I've never tasted such delicious pasta. _____

4 I can't sing the high **note**. _____

5 He owns a **chain** of hardware stores. _____

6 She hit a brilliant **service** and won the game. _____

I Following up cross-references

1.11 Look for the cross-references in these entries to answer these questions.

1 Where can you find a picture of a **pressure cooker**?

2 Where is the definition of **racoon**?

3 Where can you find out what a **rarebit** is?

4 What is the word usually used in Britain for a **letter opener**?

5 What is another word for **politics**, the subject of study?

6 Where can you find the meaning of **radii**?

7 What verb does the form **woven** come from?

8 Of which verb is **flew** the past tense?

9 Where can you find out what **laughing gas** is?

10 What is a shorter way of saying **gate money**?

11 Can you find the definition of the idiom **separate the men from the boys** at the entry for **separate**, **men**, **man**, or **boy**?

12 Where can you find the definition of the idiom **rake sb over the coals**?

13 Where can you look up an expression with a related meaning to **restraining order**?

14 Where can you find a note about words like **yell**?

2 The parts of an entry

A Information about the headword

2.1 Test yourself on the headword information in the entries.

1 What is another way of spelling **dispatch**? _____

2 What part of speech is **disparage**? _____

3 Is it a formal or an informal word? _____

4 What is the chemical symbol for **strontium**? _____

5 What is the difference between the British and the American pronunciation of **park**? _____

6 What would a **packed lunch** be called in American English? _____

7 What is the abbreviation for **ounce**? _____

8 What is **AC** the abbreviation for? _____

9 In which meaning can it also be written **ac** or **a/c**? _____

10 How is **Mr** usually written in American English? _____

11 What is another way of saying **tonne**? _____

12 **Inverted commas** is another way of saying what? _____

B Abbreviations

2.2 Check that you know what the abbreviations stand for by filling in the words in full in this crossword. Then rearrange the letters in the circles to find the word that is abbreviated to **prep.**

Across
1 pt
4 adj.
6 symb
8 det.
9 pp
11 conj.

Down
2 sb
3 pl.
5 abbr.
6 sth
7 adv.
10 pron.

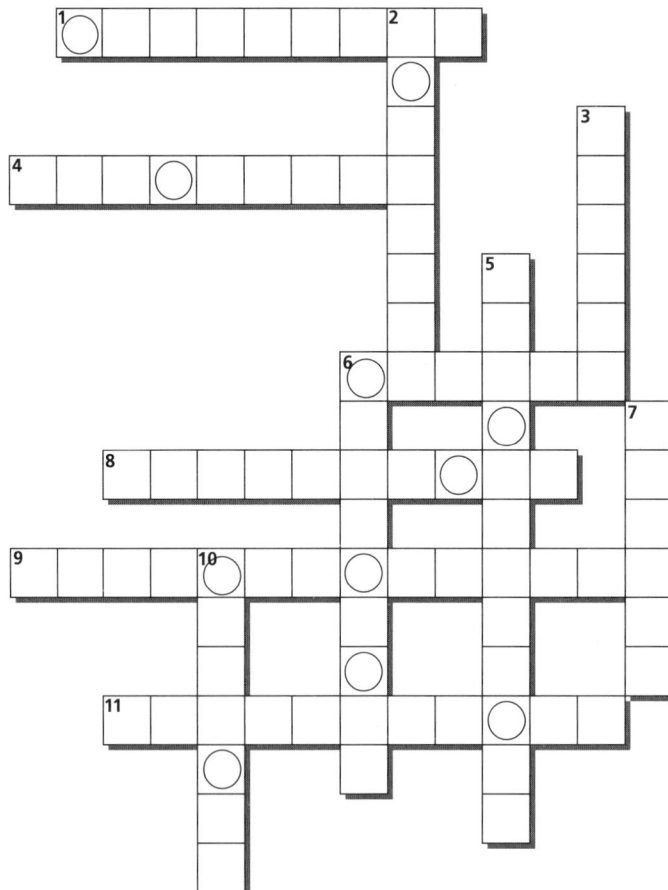

C Idioms

2.3 Answer these questions by looking at the **IDM** section of the entries for the words in **bold**.

1 At the entry **bare**, how many idioms can you find for the adjective? _____

2 How many for the verb **bare**? _____

3 In which entry can you find the idiom **not at any price**? _____

4 At the entry for shot, under which part of speech will you find the idiom **shot through with sth**? _____

5 Under which part of speech will you find the idiom **a shot in the arm**? _____

6 Is it correct to say *this will fill the bill?* and *this will fit the bill?* _____

D Phrasal verbs

2.4 Answer these questions by looking at the **PHR V** section of the entries for the words in **bold**.

1 What phrasal verb is formed with the verb **beef**? _____

2 How many phrasal verbs are formed with **wake**? _____

3 What phrasal verb is formed with the verb **peter**? _____

4 What is the meaning of **hold forth**? _____

5 **Hold sth on** means to keep something _____ .

6 How many meanings can you find for **hold sb to sth**? _____

E Derivatives

2.5 Write down the entries where you can find these words.

bafflement, baffling _____   epidemic (*adj.*) _____

destabilization _____   greenness _____

deterrence _____   magenta (*noun*) _____

drowsily, drowsiness _____   racketeering _____

F Examples

2.6 Look at the examples in the entries for the words in **bold** to find the answers to these questions.

1 Which is correct: *Blue suits you* or *You suit blue*? (**suit**)

2 If something *makes your heart ache*, how do you feel? _____

3 What would you expect to see on a tourist **trail**? _____

4 If something is not being used, you can say it is _____ _____ (**dust**).

5 A person of *no fixed abode* has no permanent _____ .

6 Which is correct: *The movie was shot on location* or *in location?* (**location**)

G Help

2.7 Look at the help notes for the words in **bold**, then correct the mistakes in these sentences.

1 **Ask** to her what's wrong.

2 I don't want to play no more. (**any more**)

3 Every individual's fingerprints are very **unique**.

4 Can you please **explain** me the problem?

5 I've been waiting for the bus **since** half an hour.

6 My new TV has **a** LCD screen.

7 The headmaster wanted to know what I was doing? (**indirect question**)

8 Can you **suggest** us a good restaurant?

3 Looking at definitions

A It's a type of...

3.1 Match up the items on the left with something from the list on the right. Say what you think the things are. Then read the definitions in the dictionary and see whether you were right.

It's a type of... It's a kind of...

American football	vegetable
Chinese cabbage	illness
French horn	dog
German measles	cake
Afghan hound	sport
Danish pastry	musical instrument
Turkish delight	sweet/candy

3.2 Check that you know the meaning of the words in the box and then decide which fits best into the sentences below.

> machine   quality   organization   instrument   act   substance   device   state   process
> container   tool   feeling

1 A vat is a large _____ for holding liquids.

2 A stapler is a small _____ for putting staples into paper.

3 A stethoscope is an _____ that a doctor uses to listen to sb's heart and breathing.

4 A chisel is a _____ used for shaping wood, stone or metal.

5 A blender is an electric _____ for mixing soft food or liquid.

6 Gel is a thick _____ like jelly.

7 Desalination is the _____ of removing salt from sea water.

8 Horror is a _____ of great shock, fear or disgust.

9 Wealth is the _____ of being rich.

10 Beauty is the _____ of being pleasing to the senses or to the mind.

11 A trade union is an _____ of workers that exists to protect their interests.

12 Ambush is the _____ of making a surprise attack on someone.

3.3 Put the words in the box into the right categories.

> lava   glider   satin   haggis   ozone   tikka   helium   venom   SUV   ingot
> microlight   tweed   rickshaw   wax

vehicle	*aircraft*	*dish*	*cloth*	*solid*	*liquid*	*gas*
_____	_____	_____	_____	_____	_____	_____
_____	_____	_____	_____	_____	_____	_____

B Adjectives often used in definitions

3.4 Check the meanings of the adjectives in the box, and then choose the ones that you think best describe the nouns below. You should choose at least two adjectives for each noun.

> thin   thick   flat   pale   round   long   rough   smooth   hollow   pointed
> small   sharp   shiny   soft   light

1 disk	_____ _____	4 cream	_____ _____
2 satin	_____ _____	5 tube	_____ _____
3 thorn	_____ _____	6 tweed	_____ _____

4 Looking at examples

A What examples can tell you

4.1 Use the examples in the dictionary to find this information.

1 Look at the entry for **advice** and find:
   a four verbs that are used with it. _____
   b two professional groups that you could go to for advice. _____
   c two expressions that mean 'some advice'. _____

2 Look at **perfume**.
   a In what type of container is perfume sold? _____
   b Where in a shop can you buy perfume? _____
   c Is it possible to talk about the **perfume** of flowers? _____

3 Look at **launch**.
   a What can be launched into space? _____
   b What weapons can be launched into the air or sea? _____
   c What other types of things can you launch? _____

4 Look at **bitter** (*adjective*).
   a What nouns to do with weather are used with **bitter**? _____
   b What feelings can be described as **bitter**? _____
   c Can a person be **bitter**? _____

B Figurative examples

4.2 Look at these figurative examples and explain to a partner why the expressions in them were chosen. It may help to reread the definitions of the literal meanings of the words in **bold**.

1 **infectious** laughter
2 She had a will of **iron**.
3 **mouth-watering** travel brochures
4 The building is a **maze** of corridors.
5 He **replayed** the scene in his mind.
6 That car of yours should really have been **pensioned** off years ago.

C Collocations in examples

4.3 In these sentences, replace the part in *italics* with a common expression which means the same. The words you will need are all in the box. If you need help, look at the entries for the word in **bold**.

a	a	a	**ability**	best	days	have	in	make	**murmur**
music	my	**nice**	**note**	**novelty**	of	of	of	**old**	out
set	**sight**	the	the	time	to	to	value	without	

1 She accepted the decision *without protesting*. _____
2 The words were *made into a song* by Schubert. _____
3 I hope you *enjoy yourself* at your friend's. _____
4 Let me *write down* your address. _____
5 They didn't have television *many years ago*. _____
6 I'll do it *as well as I can*. _____
7 We waved until they were *too far away for us to see*. _____
8 I suppose it has a certain *attraction because it is new*. _____

5 Looking at notes

A Which word?

5.1 In this paragraph there are eight mistakes that the writer could have avoided if he had read the notes about the words. Can you correct his errors?

At the weekend, I lastly had the chance to see a play that I had been wanting to see for long. I am very interesting in the theatre, and my friend was playing the leading role. Afterwards I met my friend and complemented him on his performance, specially his amazing calmness. He said me that when he first started acting he was used to get very nervous, but now he was less effected by nerves.

➔ You can find a list of these **Which word?** notes on page R93 of your dictionary.

B Vocabulary building

5.2 Choose a better word in each sentence to replace the word in **bold**.

1 During the war they had to live in **bad** conditions. _____
2 There was a **bad** smell coming from the drains. _____
3 He was involved in a **bad** accident and **broke** both legs. _____
4 When we arrived, a **good** meal was waiting for us, and the **smell** of coffee wafted out of the kitchen. _____
5 On holiday last summer we had **nice** weather. _____
6 She always wears very **nice** clothes. _____
7 How many **pieces** of bread would you like? _____
8 I'd like to mention a related **thing**. _____
9 Her optimism's a **thing** she's inherited from her mother. _____
10 What **things** do the exam questions cover? _____

C Grammar notes

5.3 Put these words in order to make good grammatical sentences. You will find a grammar note to help you at the entry for the word in **bold**.

1 **enjoy**/we/much/playing/very/tennis
   _____ .

2 **half**/had/an/in/wait/the/hour/I/to/queue
   _____ .

3 **used**/our/go/Wales/to/holidays/we/to/for
   _____ .

4 **much**/much/but/don't/house/I/I/love/my/spend/there/time/very
   _____ .

5 **one**/Henry's/was/old/the
   _____ .

5.4 Complete these sentences with a suitable word.

1 I **wish** I _____ where he's got to.
2 He was **sit**ting _____ a hard wooden chair _____ his desk.
3 **None** of the music they play _____ very modern.
4 We really **enjoyed** _____ on holiday.

6 Looking at illustrations

A Objects from around the world

6.1 These objects come from all over the world. What are they and where do they come from? Check your answers by looking in your dictionary.

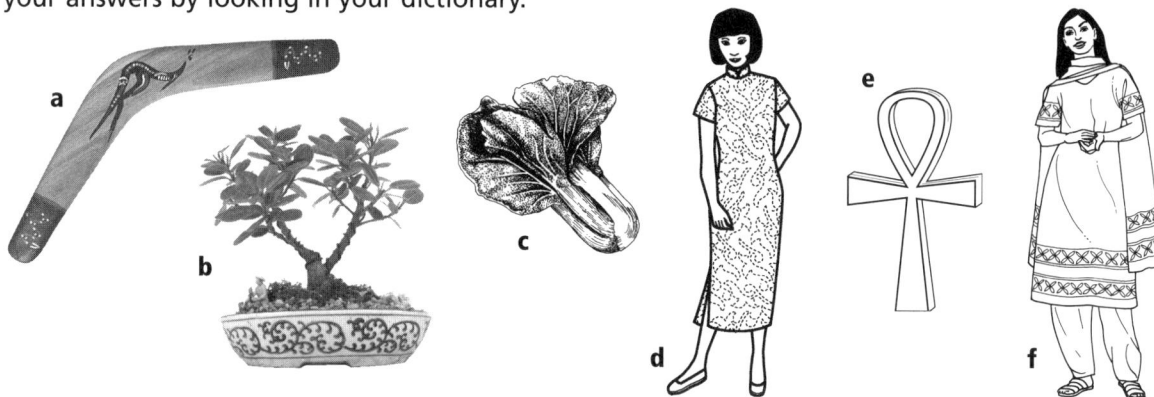

	picture	What is it?	Where is it from?
1 boomerang	a	_____	_____
2 ankh	_____	_____	_____
3 pak choi	_____	_____	_____
4 cheongsam	_____	_____	_____
5 bonsai	_____	_____	_____
6 salwar kameez	_____	_____	_____

B Adjectives

6.2 This illustration shows the differences between three adjectives used to talk about damage. Match each definition to the correct word and picture. Check your answers by looking at the definitions for **broken**, **chipped** and **cracked**.

1	damaged with lines in its surface, but not completely broken	**broken**
2	that has been damaged or injured; no longer whole or working correctly	**chipped**
3	that has been damaged by a small piece breaking off	**cracked**

6.3 The following words are used to refer to different types of line. Write an adjective from the box which describes the type of line, then look at the illustration at **line** in your dictionary to check your answers.

vertical	horizontal	diagonal
straight	wavy/wiggly	curved
dotted	parallel	zigzag

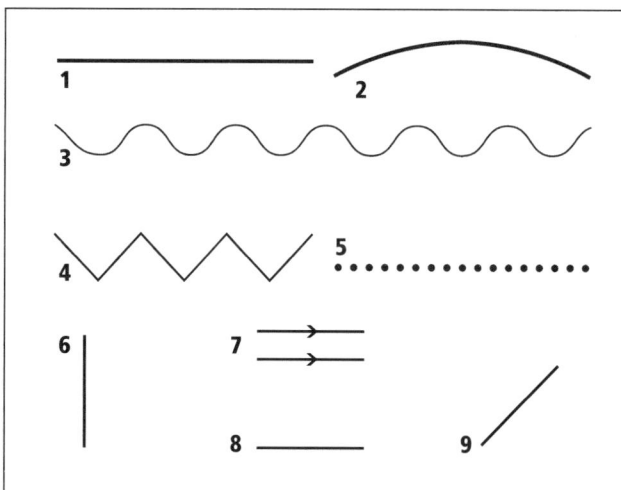

1	_____	6	_____
2	_____	7	_____
3	_____	8	_____
4	_____	9	_____
5	_____		

C Verbs

squeeze

crush

squash

press

6.4 Look at the illustrations to choose the most suitable verb to complete the sentences. You will find the answers in the examples at the entries for **squeeze**, **crush**, **squash** and **press**.

    1 to _____ a button / switch / key

    2 to _____ a tube of toothpaste

    3 The tomatoes at the bottom of the bag had been _____ .

    4 They _____ the olives with a heavy wooden press.

6.5 What else can you **squeeze**, **crush**, **squash** and **press**? Choose the best word to complete these sentences. Use the entries in your dictionary to help you.

    1 _____ here to start the washing machine.

    2 Ryan's sister _____ some fresh juice for him.

    3 Carry your sandwiches in a box so that you don't _____ them.

    4 Pete _____ a clove of garlic and put it in the frying pan.

6.6 These words are all quite similar in meaning. Look at the pictures below and write the word or expression after the definition.

crawling

squatting

kneeling

crouching

on her hands and knees

    1 sitting on your heels with your knees bent up close to your body: _____

    2 moving forward on your hands and knees, with your body close to the ground: _____

    3 putting your body close to the ground by bending your legs under you: _____

    4 supporting your body on your knee or knees: _____

    5 supporting your body on your hands and knees: _____

D Topic vocabulary

6.7 Write down as many names of fruit and vegetables as you can think of. Then look at the illustrations on page R12–13 of your dictionary and see if there are any that you can add to your list.

6.8 Look at the pictures of musical instruments on pages R6–7 of your dictionary and find out what somebody who plays each of the following is called. You can also check by looking at or near the separate dictionary entries for musical instruments.

instrument	*player*	*instrument*	*player*
violin	_____	clarinet	_____
guitar	_____	cello	_____
piano	_____	horn	_____
oboe	_____	drum	_____
trumpet	_____	flute	_____
harp	_____	bass	_____

7 Pronunciation

A Phonetic transcriptions

7.1 Which of these words begin with the sound /tʃ/ and which with /k/?

chirp   chiropodist   chin   choir   chipmunk   chisel   chord   Celtic   character   cello

/tʃ/   /k/

_____   _____   _____   _____

_____   _____   _____   _____

_____   _____   _____   _____

7.2 Which of these pairs of words are not pronounced the same as each other?

1	wry	rye		5	phew	few
2	rein	reign		6	ail	aisle
3	knot	not		7	pallet	palate
4	known	none		8	pull	pool

7.3 Underline the consonant that is not pronounced in these words.

gnome   wrathful   honeycomb   receipt   honorary   thumbnail   castle
pseudonym   freight   indebted   palmtop

7.4 In how many different ways is the letter **g** pronounced in these words?

veg   geriatric   ginger   ageism   dungeon   margarine

7.5 Arrange these words in three columns according to the pronunciation of **gh**.

cough   thorough   ghetto   tough   though   gherkin   bough
ghost   laughter

/g/   /f/   **not pronounced**

_____   _____   _____

_____   _____   _____

_____   _____   _____

7.6 Can you work out which words these pronunciations represent?

1	/ˈʃaʊə(r)/		6	/ˈdʒestʃə(r)/
2	/ˈiːmeɪl/		7	/hɑːv; NAmE hæv/
3	/ˈtjuːtə(r)/		8	/ˈθɪŋkɪŋ/
4	/gest/		9	/ˈvɪʃəs/
5	/ˈvɪʒuəl/		10	/ˈnaɪtmeə(r); NAmE -mer/

7.7 Each of these pronunciations represents two or more different words. See how many you can find.

1	/ˈkɜːnl; NAmE ˈkɜːrnl/		6	/juː/
2	/dɪˈzɜːt; NAmE dɪˈzɜːrt/		7	/weɪl/
3	/kɔː(r)/		8	/dɪə(r); NAmE dɪr/
4	/ˈflaʊəri/		9	/təʊ; NAmE toʊ/
5	/sent/		10	/səʊ; NAmE soʊ/

7.8 Which of these words does not contain the sound /ə/?

> potato   writer   henna   cramped   business   undeterred   actually
> tractor   polar   climate

B Stress

7.9 Underline the syllable which has the main stress in these expressions.

> mixed ability   half-time   far-sightedness   eye-catching   balance sheet   sign language

7.10 Look at the transcriptions of these words and decide which of them are *not* stressed on the first syllable.

> camouflage   conclude   eliminate   eyewitness   foray   hazelnut   phenomenon
> philosophy   prevalent   spellbinding

7.11 Underline the syllable which has the main stress in these words.

1 politics   political   politician
2 photograph   photographer   photographic
3 conspire   conspiracy   conspiratorial
4 inform   informative   information
5 deport   deportee   deportation
6 celebrate   celebratory   celebration
7 educate   education   educational
8 profession   professional   professionalism

7.12 Underline the stressed syllable in the words in **bold** in these sentences.

1 Harris holds the world hundred metres **record**.
2 The band was **recorded** live in concert.
3 Would anybody **object** if I changed the date of the meeting?
4 I thought I saw a strange **object** in the sky.
5 The city was **deserted**.
6 They were lost in the **desert** for days.
7 We've made a lot of **progress** since last week.
8 Work on the new parliament building is **progressing** slowly.
9 The **conflict** was sparked by an assassination attempt.
10 I was confused by the **conflicting** advice they gave me.
11 We haven't had a chance to **perfect** the technique yet.
12 It was a **perfect** day for fishing.

→ You will find a list of all of the phonetic symbols used in transcriptions along the bottom of every page of the main A–Z section of the dictionary. In addition, full information about how pronunciation is treated in the dictionary can be found on pages R118–9.

8 Spelling

A Finding the spelling

8.1 Complete these words by looking in the dictionary.

1 Cheer up – you seem rather in the **dol**_____**ms** today.

2 I feel such a **fru**_____ ! I need to buy some new clothes.

3 Only a complete **ig**_____ would get that wrong.

4 We were all excited, but she was really **bla**_____ because she'd met him before.

5 The company made **swin**_____ cuts to salaries.

6 He's got a **myn**_____ bird that says 'I'm free!'

B Spelling variations

8.2 Some words have two possible spellings. Find the more usual spelling for the words in **bold**.

1 Have some **camomile** tea before bed – it'll help you sleep. _____

2 A holiday with her wouldn't be much fun – she's so **straight-laced**. _____

3 He's too busy **eying** up other girls to take any notice of me. _____

4 Can I borrow your **hairdrier**, please? _____

5 I've just been **focussing** on work and rather ignoring my family, I'm afraid. _____

6 I hope you don't think I'm **nosey**, but are you from Norwich? _____

7 Marco's English has **benefitted** from living with an English family. _____

8 The castle dates back to **mediaeval** times. _____

C British and American spellings

8.3 There are some differences between British and American spelling. Use the dictionary to complete the table.

British	American	Other examples
colour	color	hum_____ / hum_____, fav_____ / fav_____
_____	liter	cen_____ / cen_____, the_____ / the_____
defence	_____	lic_____ / lic_____ (*noun*), off_____ / off_____
_____	traveling	canc_____ / canc_____, ped_____ / ped_____
fulfil	_____	ski_____ / ski_____, app_____ / app_____
_____	analyze	paral_____ / paral_____, breath_____ / breath_____
_____	catalog	dia_____ / dia_____, ana_____ / ana_____

D Silent letters

8.4 Find the silent letter (or letters) in these words.

1 There's a su___tle difference between being confident and being arrogant.

2 He was indi___ted for tax evasion.

3 Try to breathe deeply using your diaphra___m.

4 The committee was ve___emently opposed to the chairman's plans.

5 He presented her with a sa___phire ring on their wedding anniversary.

6 An increasing number of children suffer from as___ma.

7 I never had any qua___ms about employing him.

8 The funeral was a solem___ affair.

E Non-standard spellings

8.5 The words in **bold** are written in non-standard spelling. Write the word with the standard spelling.

1 **Wot** a goal! _____
2 He's **gonna** have an accident one day. _____
3 I **ain't** as young as I was. _____
4 I'm tired **'cos** I went to bed late. _____
5 I **wanna** go home now. _____
6 'Where's Mum?' 'I **dunno**.' _____
7 Tell us **yer** name! _____
8 Give **'em** back! _____
9 Happy birthday. Lots of **luv** from Tracey. _____
10 **Gimme** some money and I'll go away. _____

F Sounds people make

8.6 Choose the correct exclamation for each sentence. Practise saying the sentences.

1 **Psst / Ugh**, there's a spider on my foot.
2 **Ahem! / Aha!** Now I know why you wanted to come!
3 **Um / Phew**, do you mind if I ask you a question?
4 **Tut / Hmm**, I'm not sure which one I prefer.
5 **Brrr / Sh**, it's cold in here.
6 **Uh-oh / Oi**, what do you think you're doing?

G First letters

8.7 How many words start with the following combinations of letters? (Do not include abbreviations or words with a hyphen after the first letter, e.g. **T-shirt**.)

Letter combination	None	Fewer than 10	More than 10	Sample word
aa	____	✓	____	aardvark
bw	____	____	____	_____
dh	____	____	____	_____
ee	____	____	____	_____
fy	____	____	____	_____
hw	____	____	____	_____
ie	____	____	____	_____
kw	____	____	____	_____
ly	____	____	____	_____
mn	____	____	____	_____
nm	____	____	____	_____
ps	____	____	____	_____
rw	____	____	____	_____
vr	____	____	____	_____
wr	____	____	____	_____
q + any letter except 'u'	____	____	____	_____
x	____	____	____	_____
y + any consonant	____	____	____	_____
z + any consonant	____	____	____	_____

9 Looking at verbs

A Irregular verbs

9.1 Fill in the correct forms of the verbs in these sentences.

1 Have you _____ the theatre to book the tickets? (**ring**)
2 I'm going to wear the red dress I _____ for the party last week. (**wear**)
3 He was _____ by a bee and his arm _____ up. (**sting, swell**)
4 That winter, the river _____ for the first time in ten years. (**freeze**)
5 How much money have you _____ ? (**spend**)
6 It was a lovely day and the sun _____ brightly. (**shine**)
7 Prices have _____ by 5%. (**rise**)
8 A loud bang _____ me at three in the morning. (**wake**)

B Spelling irregularities

9.2 Fill in the correct forms in these sentences.

1 They have _____ all over the world. (**travel**)
2 Why are you _____ to me? (**lie**)
3 I _____ onto the bus and sat down. (**hop**)
4 When the fire alarm went off, everyone _____ . (**panic**)
5 My doctor _____ me to a specialist. (**refer**)
6 He disguised himself by _____ his hair. (**dye**)

C Structures with verbs

9.3 Use the information in the verb codes to decide whether these sentences are acceptable ✓ or not ✗.

1 He hacked the bush.   ___✗___
2 He hacked the bush down.   _____
3 Pam handled the situation well.   _____
4 Pam always handles well in these situations.   _____
5 A bit of fresh air won't harm.   _____
6 The dog won't harm you.   _____
7 Who's parked in front of our entrance?   _____
8 Where did you park?   _____
9 They faxed us the invoice.   _____
10 Can you spare me a minute?   _____
11 Be careful with that! It cost me!   _____
12 They served us drinks in the garden.   _____

→ The verb codes are explained on pages R36–8 of the dictionary.

9.4 Delete the form of the verb which is incorrect in these sentences.

1 They are **considering** to build/building a new motorway.
2 We **expect** to arrive/arriving about two.
3 She **denied** to take/taking the money.
4 They **discussed** to change/changing the company's name.
5 He **resolved** to try/trying harder next time.
6 I couldn't **resist** to eat/eating the last biscuit.
7 Do you **miss** to see/seeing the children every day?

8 She **suggested** <u>to go</u>/<u>going</u> out for a meal.

9 I **waited** <u>to see</u>/<u>seeing</u> what he would do next.

10 He **neglected** <u>to tell</u>/<u>telling</u> us that he had no money.

9.5 Look at the patterns in the entries for the verbs in these sentences and complete them with a suitable preposition.

1 I concluded _____ his remarks that he disapproved _____ the idea.

2 They promoted him _____ assistant head _____ head.

3 The hotel provided us _____ towels and bathrobes.

4 She quarrelled _____ her brother _____ money.

5 It is good to quote _____ the text in your essay.

D Extra information about verbs

9.6 Which of these verbs is...

| bother | handicap | pain | begrudge | pardon | bulge |

1 not used in the progressive tenses?

2 usually used in the progressive tenses?

3 not usually used in the progressive tenses?

4 usually passive?

5 often used in negative sentences and questions?

6 often used in negative sentences?

E Verb phrases

9.7 Look at the entry for **get**. Use a phrase with **get** to complete the sentences.

1 I put my clothes on quickly.   I _____ quickly.

2 We were shocked when we heard the news.   We _____ when we heard the news.

3 We married in a registry office.   We _____ in a registry office.

4 I started talking to him.   I _____ to him.

5 I haven't read very much of my book.   I haven't _____ with my book.

9.8 Use the verbs in the box to complete the sentences.

| go | make | do | have | give | take |

1 We promised to help each other.   We _____ a promise to help each other.

2 Look at this!   _____ a look at this!

3 He sighed and turned away.   He _____ a sigh and turned away.

4 I like to swim before work.   I like to _____ for a swim before lunch.

5 Can you help me dig?   Can you help me _____ some digging?

6 I showered and got dressed.   I _____ a shower and got dressed.

10 Looking at nouns

A The plural of nouns

10.1 What is the plural form of these nouns?

thesis	_____	bacterium	_____
aircraft	_____	salmon	_____
crony	_____	embryo	_____
sister-in-law	_____	housewife	_____
gateau	_____	fungus	_____
criterion	_____	bottle opener	_____
deer	_____	appendix	_____

10.2 Look up the following words and find out what they have in common.

> binoculars   sunglasses   shears   swimming trunks   tongs   pliers

B Singular or plural

10.3 Which verb form is correct?

1   The graffiti **was** / **were** still visible after many years.
2   There **is** / **are** no further data available.
3   The media **has** / **have** an increasing influence on our lives.
4   **Is** / **Are** the spaghetti cooked?
5   The bacteria **is** / **are** spread by physical contact.

10.4 Which of these words are plural?

> goods   odds   news   valuables   phonetics   applause   diabetes   basics   rabies

C Singular or plural verb

10.5 Which verb form is correct?

1   The police **is** / **are** conducting a house-to-house search.
2   The government **has** / **have** banned smoking in public places.
3   The brass **has** / **have** to play very softly in this passage.
4   The orchestra **play** / **plays** without a conductor.
5   The press **has** / **have** been criticized by the organization's lawyers.
6   The crew **was** / **were** very helpful.
7   Her family **is** / **are** all musicians.
8   Congress **has** / **have** voted to change the tax laws.

D Countable and uncountable

10.6 Answer these questions.

1   Look at the entry for **tin**. What is 'tin'? What is 'a tin'?
2   Look up **bronze**. What is 'bronze'? What is 'a bronze'?
3   Now check **pottery**. What is 'pottery'? What is 'a pottery'?
4   Look at **property**. What two meanings can the plural 'properties' have?
5   The word **paper** has eight meanings in the dictionary. In which two cases can it be uncountable?

10.7 Correct or not? Look at the information given in the dictionary about the word in **bold** in these sentences and decide whether the sentences are correct or not.

   1 It was a very useful **advice**.
   2 He bought some new camping **equipment** for the holiday.
   3 As soon as we have more **informations**, we will let you know.
   4 The **furniture** are all antique.
   5 They received a set of **cutleries** as a wedding present.

E Nouns with prepositions

10.8 Fill in the correct preposition to follow these nouns

   1 She felt terrible **guilt** _____ leaving him alone.
   2 Do you have a **preference** _____ one of the options?
   3 The **preparations** _____ the wedding took months.
   4 Her **promotion** _____ managing director surprised everyone.
   5 Their **punishment** _____ breaking the rules was expulsion.
   6 There is a great deal of **pressure** _____ the team before the final.

F One of...

10.9 Complete the sentences using the correct word from the box.

grain	speck	flake	blade	piece

   1 a _____ of rice   4 a _____ of grass   6 a _____ of dust
   2 a _____ of advice   5 a _____ of clothing   7 a _____ of snow
   3 a _____ of sand

G A certain amount of...

10.10 Complete the sentences using the correct word from the box.

breath	chink	spot	flash	glimmer	gust	inch	round	shred

   1 There wasn't an _____ of space left.
   2 I had a _____ of inspiration.
   3 Let's have a _____ of applause for our guest tonight.
   4 There was a _____ of light visible beneath the door.
   5 There wasn't a _____ of evidence against him.
   6 I'm going out for a _____ of air.
   7 A _____ of wind blew her hat off.
   8 There is still a _____ of hope left.
   9 Will you stay for a _____ of lunch?

H Adjectives as nouns

10.11 Correct these sentences where necessary. Do you notice any pattern?

   1 The injureds were rushed to hospital.
   2 Not many whites live in this neighbourhood.
   3 The money will be used to help the poors.
   4 The blonds usually have to be careful in the sun.
   5 The TV studio was invaded by a bunch of crazy.
   6 The new scheme is designed to help dyslexics.

11 Looking at adjectives

A Adjectives in comparisons

11.1 Check the entries for these words and find the comparative and superlative forms.

nice	_____	_____	foggy	_____	_____
tidy	_____	_____	lucky	_____	_____
hot	_____	_____	good	_____	_____
cruel	_____	_____	bad	_____	_____
dense	_____	_____	far	_____	_____

B Adjectives with nouns

11.2 Match these adjectives with the nouns they go with.

wavy   finance
a sharp   hair
a steady   question
a rhetorical   boyfriend
solid   beach
a mixed-up   gold
high   distinction
chubby   cyclone
a secluded   teenager
a devastating   cheeks

11.3 Look up the entries for the adjectives in these sentences and decide whether they have been used correctly.

1 They tiptoed past the **asleep** guard.
2 Which problem is **chief**?
3 The pilot survived the crash **unscathed**.
4 It was a **flagrant** abuse of the rules.
5 The solution is just **interim**.
6 The **afraid** children hid in the cellar.
7 The trip was a **downright** disaster.
8 There was an **alone** tree on the horizon.

C Adjectives with prepositions

11.4 Decide which preposition in the box fits into these sentences. You will have to use some of them more than once.

| about | at | of | to | with |

1 I'm optimistic _____ the future.
2 He was content _____ his life there.
3 I was wrong _____ that girl – she's actually very nice.
4 Is he still mad _____ me?
5 We are open _____ suggestions.
6 I'm not convinced _____ it.
7 She's proud _____ her achievements.
8 Weekly payments are preferable _____ monthly ones.

12 Idioms

A Sayings

12.1 These are all common sayings. Can you guess the missing words? Try to fill the gaps before you look in the dictionary. Is there a similar saying in your language?

1 Like father, like __son__ .
2 Two heads are better than _____ .
3 Boys will be _____ .
4 Easy come, easy _____ .
5 First come, first _____ .

6 Practice makes _____ .
7 Time is _____ .
8 Where there's a will, there's a _____ .
9 Don't judge a book by its _____ .
10 The end justifies the _____ .

12.2 The idioms below can be used in short versions as well as their full versions. Match the beginnings with the correct ends.

1 Two's company,
2 An eye for an eye
3 Fools rush in
4 Where there's life,
5 He who hesitates
6 It's an ill wind
7 The proof of the pudding
8 When in Rome,
9 The spirit is willing,
10 Birds of a feather

a but the flesh is weak.
b three's a crowd.
c is in the eating.
d and a tooth for a tooth.
e is lost.
f flock together.
g where angels fear to tread.
h that blows nobody any good.
i do as the Romans do.
j there's hope.

B Expressions used in particular circumstances

12.3 Decide which is the correct idiom here. What expression is used…

1 to say that you don't know something?
I ask you! / Don't ask me!

2 when somebody has thanked you?
You're welcome! / Please yourself!

3 to say that something isn't very likely?
You bet! / Don't bet on it!

4 when you think that somebody has asked a silly question?
Do me a favour! / No kidding!

5 to tell somebody that what they were hoping for is not very likely?
Watch this space! / In your dreams!

6 to remind somebody that you warned them about this?
I told you so! / Eat your heart out!

7 to encourage people and to tell them they are doing something right?
That's an idea! / That's the idea!

8 to ask the reason for something?
How come? / How long have you got?

9 to say that you don't want to talk about something?
Don't mention it! / Let's not even go there!

10 when something is starting to happen?
Here you go! / Here we go!

11 to ask whether somebody is interested in something?
How does that grab you? / What are you like?

13 Phrasal verbs

A New phrasal verbs

13.1 These phrasal verbs have recently become common, or recently acquired new meanings. Can you fit them into the sentences below? (You may need to alter the form to make the correct tense.)

> feed into   walk through   crash out   beat yourself up   scope out
> click through   zone out   cut up

1   It's happened now. Don't _____ about it.
2   From our homepage you can _____ to read other articles.
3   The British number one has _____ in the first round of the championships.
4   All these ideas _____ the development of the new product.
5   When we finally arrived back at the hostel, everyone _____ .
6   Can you just _____ me _____ what I have to do again?
7   And then this red sports car _____ me _____ on the bypass...
8   We'll have to _____ the project before we can estimate the time it'll take.

B Word order

13.2 Read the section on pages R40–1 of your dictionary about the grammar of phrasal verbs, then insert the words in brackets into these sentences in the correct place.

1   Can you copy in on your email (*me*)?
2   We checked into (*the hotel*).
3   Can I phone in (*my order*)?
4   Give me the parcel. I have to pass by on my way home. (*the post office*)
5   She turned off (*the light that had been shining in her eyes*).
6   They want to chop down (*that old oak tree*).
7   The report singled out as the key figure in the affair (*him*).
8   You've missed out (*an m in accommodation*).

C Travel and computers

13.3 Look at these phrasal verbs and check their meanings in the dictionary. Then put them into the travel or the computers category.

> check into sth   drill down   fall over   take off   scan sth in   touch down   stop over   back
> sth up   jack into sth   get away   set off   log off

computers

_____   _____   _____

_____   _____   _____

travel

_____   _____   _____

_____   _____   _____

D The meaning of particles

13.4 Decide which meaning **up** has with these verbs: movement upwards, 'increasing', or 'improving'.

> ratchet sth up   juice sth up   dig sth up   hoover sth up   spruce up   step sth up

movement: _____ _____

increase: _____ _____

improve: _____ _____

14 Synonyms and opposites

A Synonyms

14.1 Look up the word in column A and match it with the word in column B that is closest to it in meaning. You will find synonyms given in the dictionary after the symbol **SYN** .

A	B
preposterous	dishearten
egocentric	individually
dramatist	luckily
synthetic	outrageous
singly	playwright
fortunately	project
demoralize	man-made
jut	selfish

14.2 Look at the note at **cheap**. Complete these sentences using each of the words once.

> cheap   competitive   budget   reasonable   inexpensive

1   I don't like that one. It looks _____ .
2   What about this one? It looks nice and the price is _____.
3   We offer a quality service at a _____ price.
4   The brochure has a great range of luxury, family and _____ hotels.
5   Can you recommend a good, _____ hotel?

14.3 Look at the note at **trip**. Complete these sentences using each of the words once.

> trip   journey   tour   expedition   excursions

1   What are you doing for your holiday? We're going on a coach _____ of Belgium.
2   There will be plenty of opportunities for making _____ from the cruise ship.
3   She's leading a scientific _____ in the Himalayas.
4   It was a long _____, over difficult terrain.
5   I've got another business _____ at the end of the month.

14.4 In four of these sentences, **think** can be replaced by another verb or phrase. Look at the note at **think** and choose the most suitable replacement. In one sentence, **think** is the best choice. You may need to change the form of the verb.

> believe   feel   reckon   be under the impression that

1   I think that it is wrong to eat meat. _____
2   I think we're going to win this tournament! _____
3   I think that we should tell the police. _____
4   I thought that you hated big parties. _____
5   What do you think? The red one or the green one? _____

14.5 Some of the following sentences are correct, but some contain a wrong choice of word. In each case, decide whether the sentence is correct or not. If not, say which near synonym would be a better choice. Use the *Synonyms* notes for the words in brackets to help you.

1   I had a terrible *fright* of failure. (**fear**)
2   I was never any good at playing the trumpet for the *simple* reason that I never practised. (**plain**)
3   The court *announced* that the strike action was illegal. (**declare**)

4　The failure of the company was a direct *result* of bad management. (**effect**)

5　I would strongly *recommend* against going out on your own. (**recommend**)

6　Badly fed children suffer a lot of minor *diseases*. (**disease**)

7　I've *checked* the calculations and they are all quite correct. (**check**)

8　They were trying to navigate with a hopelessly *incorrect* map. (**wrong**)

9　Go *outside* and see if it is raining. (**outside**)

10　The minister refused to *remark* on the allegations made against him. (**comment**)

14.6　The following sentences are not wrong, but in each case there is a better word that you could choose instead. Look at the notes at the words in **bold** for help.

1　Crowds gathered to **complain** about the police violence.

2　The police had tried to **frighten** him into signing a confession.

3　My feet were **hurt**ing after the long walk.

4　Caring for **old** relatives can be both stressful and rewarding.

5　It's a farm shop, selling meat and cheese and other fresh **product**s.

6　We had to call somebody out to **pull** our car to a garage.

7　There seemed to be no clear **reason** for the attack.

8　I've got a lot of boring domestic **task**s to do today.

9　It's a joke. Didn't you **understand** it?

10　Somebody tried to make a **funny** remark which fell flat.

B　Opposites

14.7　In each line of the table, four out of the five words form their opposites with the same prefix. Which one is different? You will find opposites given after the symbol **OPP**.

1　mature　mortal　plausible　practical　relevant

2　advantage　agree　approve　comfortable　contented

3　convincing　fortunately　intentional　logical　manageable

4　competent　efficient　excusable　flammable　sincere

5　alcoholic　fiction　remarkable　renewable　returnable

14.8　Complete the following sentences using opposites from exercise 14.7. In some cases, more than one answer is possible.

1　I strongly ＿＿＿＿＿ with her views on education.

2　We still rely too heavily on ＿＿＿＿＿ sources of energy.

3　Such behaviour is ＿＿＿＿＿. We cannot allow it.

4　I found his argument wholly ＿＿＿＿＿.

5　This method is really wasteful and ＿＿＿＿＿.

14.9　Using this information in the entries, decide which of these words *cannot* be made into their opposites by adding **un-**.

> convincing　logical　fortunately　relevant　ambiguous　efficient　intentional
> flammable

14.10　What prefix can you put in front of all of these words to turn them into the opposite meaning?

> embark　mount　please　obey

15 Collocations

A What are collocations?

15.1 Look at the entry for **chance**, *noun*, sense 1.

   1 What does *a slim chance* mean?

   2 What two other expressions have almost the same meaning?

   3 Arrange these 'chances' in order from the least to the greatest: *a slim chance, no chance, a very good chance, a fifty-fifty chance.*

15.2 Look at the entry for **hope**, *noun*, sense 1. Find collocations in **bold** that express the following meanings.

   1 'to start to hope' (two ways) _____

   2 'to feel very hopeful about something' _____

   3 'to stop feeling hope' _____

   4 'to continue to feel hopeful in spite of being in a bad situation' _____

   5 'a very small amount of hope' _____

15.3 Look at the entry for **word**, *noun*, sense 1. Try to explain, in your own words, what the following collocations mean.

   1 in your own words   3 find the words

   2 in all senses of the word   4 is not the word for it

B Adverbs

15.4 Match an adverb in column A with the word it collocates with in column B. Look at the entries for the words in column A for help.

A	B
bitterly	advise
flatly	cold
highly	confidential
immensely	miss
narrowly	powerful
painfully	productive
strictly	refuse
strongly	slow

C Adjective + noun

15.5 Find an adjective that collocates with all of the nouns in each line of the table below.

_____	rain	traffic	defeat	heart	smoker
_____	wind	smell	views	language	probability
_____	cost	heel	hopes	summer	society
_____	frost	drop	wit	relief	contrast
_____	accent	grin	hint	spread	generalization

15.6 Take one pair of words from each line of the table in exercise 15.5 and complete these sentences.

   1 _____ _____ is causing major delays on all routes.

   2 Warning: this programme contains scenes of violence and _____ _____ .

   3 He has _____ _____ of becoming a professional footballer.

   4 There had been a _____ _____ overnight and the ground was frozen hard.

   5 He spoke with a _____ Scots _____ .

D Verb + noun

15.7 Complete each of the following sentences with one of the following verbs: **do**, **make**, **have**, **give**, **take**. You may need to change the form of the verb. In one case two of the verbs are possible. Look up the entries for the nouns in **bold** to help you.

1 Thank you. It's been a pleasure to _____ **business** with you.

2 Go on! _____ a **try**.

3 Go on! _____ it a **try**.

4 We need to _____ a **decision** about the venue for the conference.

5 Wow! I really think you _____ an **impression** on the judges.

6 He _____ a short **laugh**, but didn't say anything.

7 Did you _____ a **note** of the address?

8 Did you _____ **notes** at the lecture?

9 She just loves _____ **advice**, especially when it isn't wanted.

10 Do you want to _____ a **swap**?

15.8 Decide whether these sentences are correct or not, and correct them if they are wrong. Use the entries for the nouns in **bold** to help you.

1 He *dropped his **head*** in shame when they found out.

2 Her ***face* fell** when she heard the news.

3 I saw them holding **hands** in the park.

4 *Rub your **feet*** on the mat before you come in!

5 *He put his **back*** out digging the garden.

6 'I don't know', she said, *hugging her **shoulders***.

7 I slipped on the bottom step and *strained my **ankle***.

8 I *pulled a **muscle*** doing aerobics.

E Phrases

15.9 Match the heads and tails of these phrases linked by **and**. Use the entries for the words in **bold** to help you.

aims and	bustle
bribery and	cheerful
bright and	corruption
hustle and	hard
long and	objectives
push and	regulations
really and	save
rules and	shove
scrimp and	truly

15.10 Complete these sentences using the phrases from exercise 15.9. You may need to change the forms of the verbs.

1 He was forced to resign over allegations of _____ and _____.

2 They _____ and _____ to send their children to college.

3 Want to escape from the _____ and _____ of city life?

4 We thought _____ and _____ about this decision and are convinced that this is the right thing to do.

5 Before you start on a project you need to be clear about your _____ and _____.

6 I'm sick of all these _____ and _____. I want to be free to do things the way I want.

7 People were _____ and _____ to get to the exits.

8 What are you looking so _____ and _____ about this morning?

9 Do you mean what you just said? _____ and _____?

16 Compounds

A Compound nouns

16.1 Look at these definitions for compound words. What is being referred to in each case? For help, look up the words in **bold** and entries that are close to them. Notice whether the compound is spelled with one word, two words, or with a hyphen.

1 a cup for drinking **tea** _teacup_

2 a machine for making **coffee** _____

3 a bird which lives near the **sea** _____

4 a type of football (soccer) played with **five** players on each team _____

5 a bus which has two floors (**double**) _____

6 a warm bag for **sleeping** in _____

7 windows that have two layers of glass (**double**) _____

8 a fish that lives in the **sea** _____

16.2 Match a word in the first column to a word in the second column to make a compound. Which of them can refer to a person?

soap	tiger
drama	seeker
ski	shirt
sniffer	opera
stuffed	dog
asylum	queen
paper	jump

16.3 Explain what these objects are used for.

1 a bottle opener: _A bottle opener is used for opening bottles._

2 an answering machine: _____

3 a shoehorn: _____

4 a clothes horse: _____

5 a petrol pump/gas pump: _____

6 a paper clip: _____

16.4 What do you call...

1 a person who tunes **pianos**? _____

2 a man who **fishes** for a living? _____

3 a man or a woman who fights **fires**? _____

4 a person who makes **glass** objects by blowing through a tube? _____

5 a person who cleans **windows**? _____

B Compound adjectives

16.5 Give the compound adjective which can be used to describe these people.

1 A person who has a **soft** heart is _soft-hearted_.

2 A person who has a **sharp** tongue is _____.

3 A person who has an **open** mind is _____.

4 A person who can see as well as an **eagle** is _____.

5 A person who has **fair** hair is _____.

6 A person who has a **soft** voice is _____.

17 Register in language

A Register labels

17.1 Read the information about labels inside the front cover of your dictionary to find out what it means if you see these labels with a word.

formal   literary   informal   technical   slang   spoken   humorous   ironic

17.2 Now look up these expressions and find out which of these labels applies to each of them.

grizzled   _____

culture vulture   _____

big deal!   _____

execrable   _____

get a load of sth _____

recce   _____

yo   _____

alluvial   _____

B Formal and informal

17.3 Look up these words, which all mean 'small', and decide which of them are more formal and which are less formal than **small**.

tiddly   *less formal*

diminutive   _____

teensy-weensy   _____

titchy   _____

infinitesimal   _____

wee   _____

17.4 Put these words meaning 'good' in order of formality, starting with the least formal ones and ending with the most formal.

ace   _____

cracking   _____

wondrous   _____

outstanding _____

mega   _____

sublime   _____

gnarly   __1__

brill   _____

neat   _____

excellent   _____

17.5 Look at these sentences and decide whether the word in **bold** is appropriate for the context or not.

1   (*In a company report*) The new product has been a **ginormous** success.
2   (*In an email to a friend*) Wasn't that a **calamitous** storm last night?
3   (*In a chat to a colleague*) John seems really **fed up** at the moment.
4   (*In an article in a medical journal*) There were **humongous** lesions on the skin.

C Informal alternatives

17.6 In these sentences, replace the formal word with a more informal one that has the same meaning.

1 I passed my **mathematics** exam. _____

2 I'd like to get a job in **administration**. _____

3 We saw **chimpanzees, hippopotamuses** and **rhinoceroses** at the zoo. _____

4 I'm going into hospital for a small **operation**. _____

5 We need some **information** about the new arrivals. _____

6 Do you like my new **sunglasses**? _____

17.7 What parts of the body do these informal expressions refer to?

pins   hands
tootsies   ear
choppers   legs
ticker   toes
mitts   heart
shell-like   teeth

D Attitude

17.8 Read these sentences and look up the word in **bold** to help you decide whether the writer had a positive or a critical attitude.

1 She took a **childlike** pleasure in playing with the puppy.

2 He always found her manner **infantile**.

3 My grandmother was **thrifty** and always mended her old clothes.

4 He remembered his father's **penny-pinching** ways.

5 The **antiquated** equipment had been there since the factory opened.

6 There was an **old-world** feel to the hotel.

7 The newcomers were young and **brash**.

8 The warriors were **fearless** in battle.

9 They've given the job to a computer **whizz-kid**.

10 My brother is a real computer **nerd**.

E Good or bad?

17.9 Do these expressions imply a positive or a critical attitude?

1 This place rocks. _____

2 What a cool kid! _____

3 Her visit was a real downer. _____

4 He's a top bloke. _____

5 I cook a mean curry! _____

6 That guy is fit. _____

7 You look buff in those shorts. _____

8 She is a babe. _____

18 English around the world

A Varieties of English

18.1 What do the following abbreviations stand for? Check your answers inside the front cover of the dictionary.

NAmE	_____	*IrishE*	_____	*NZE*	_____
US	_____	*AustralE*	_____	*IndE*	_____
BrE	_____	*SAfrE*	_____	*NEngE*	_____
ScotE	_____	*SEAsianE*	_____		

18.2 Now look up these words and find out in which part of the world they are commonly used.

outwith	_____	cobber	_____	frogmarch	_____
checkers	_____	lakh	_____	beltway	_____

18.3 Where in the world are the following sentences most likely to be spoken?

1 Eina! That really hurt me. _____
2 We got off the bus at the motor park. _____
3 Call the computer wallah and ask him to come. _____
4 We were all in the pub for a night's crack. _____
5 We've got some hard yakka ahead of us. _____
6 He's moving into a new bachelor next week. _____
7 She looked absolutely tamping. _____
8 Children were playing soccer in the void deck. _____
9 I want to say thank you to my mwalimu. _____
10 Kia ora, my friends! _____
11 Och, it's nae as dreich as yesterday. _____

➜ You will find more information about varieties of English on page R91 of your dictionary.

B British and American English

18.4 Look up these words and fill in the table.

American spelling	British spelling	American spelling	British spelling
_____	centre	_____	plough
humor	_____	armor	_____
_____	analogue	_____	defence
esthetic	_____	maneuver	_____
_____	analyse	_____	medallist
mustache	_____	instill	_____

18.5 Use the notes at **rubbish, purse, platform, holiday** and **floor** to decide whether these statements are true ✓ or false ✗.

1 *Garbage* is the word American speakers use when British speakers say *rubbish*.
2 A *purse* in America is the same as a *handbag* in Britain.
3 An American speaker could ask 'Is this the right *platform* for the train to Chicago?'
4 Some American friends might tell you about their *holiday* in Florida in July.
5 An elderly British lady who can't walk upstairs very well would ask for a room on the *first floor*.

18.6 What do the following words have in common?

rummage sale   larder   bespoke   cougar   clear-out   specialty   snicker   off-putting

C British and American pronunciation

18.7 Look up these words and find out how the o sound is pronounced in British and North American English.

hot   dog   boat   bought

18.8 Now look up these entries and find out which part of these words is pronounced differently in American from British English.

optimist   sallow   fastener   astute   dogma   voluntary   paternal

18.9 Underline the part of the word which has the main stress a) in British English and b) in American English.

in British English	in American English
glacé	glacé
laboratory	laboratory
perfume	perfume
decor	decor

➔ You will find more information about British and American English on page R90 of your dictionary.

D Words from other languages

18.10 The following words are used in English, but come from other languages. Can you say what languages they come from?

machismo	_____	mese	_____
gesundheit	_____	ergo	_____
crescendo	_____	soupçon	_____
haiku	_____	favela	_____
wok	_____	babushka	_____

E Dishes of the world quiz

18.11 Where do these types of food come from originally? You can check your answers in the dictionary.

moussaka	Pakistan
nachos	the US
tempura	North Africa
haggis	India
balti	Scotland
mealies	France
couscous	Greece
vindaloo	South Africa
grits	Mexico
cassoulet	Japan

19 The Oxford 3000™

A Keywords

19.1 Look at the extract from *OALD* (right) and answer the questions.

1   What differences do you notice between the entries **website** and **wedding** and the others?

2   Why do you think the two entries are highlighted in this way?

3   Why do you think **wed** and **wedded** are not highlighted?

4   How many compounds with **wedding** are mentioned in the extract?

B Find a word

19.2 Find a word from the *Oxford 3000* which fits both sentences in each of these pairs.

1   You shouldn't be so _____ on yourself.

It was _____ to understand her.

2   What is the _____ of carrying on?

At that _____ I decided to leave.

3   Which country will be the next to send a man into _____?

I found a parking _____ in front of the school.

4   That is the _____ of rudeness!

The width of the cupboard is greater than the _____.

5   I had a _____ as a taxi driver when I was younger.

How do you _____ your surname?

6   Do you think we can all _____ into the car?

_____ two lemons and add the juice to the mixture.

C High-frequency words

19.3 Answer these questions about the high-frequency verb **say**.

1   **Say** is a verb. But what other parts of speech can it be? _____

2   Is the exclamation **say** formal or informal? Where is it used: in Britain or the US?

3   Which is normal in a story: *'Hello!' said I* or *'Hello!' I said*?

4   Is the vowel sound in **say** the same as the vowel sound in **said**? _____

5   If you agree strongly with someone, you can say *you can say that* _____.

6   Is it correct to say *They say her to be a hard worker*? _____

7   Which is correct: *She said me the news* or *She told me the news*?

8   Where is the idiom *you can't say fairer than that* used: in Britain or the US?

19.4 Answer these questions about the high-frequency noun **time**.

1   **Time** is a noun. But what other part of speech can it be? _____

2   If something happens at the wrong time, you can say it was _____ *timed*.

3   How do you ask someone the time according to their watch? _____

4   Which is correct: *We arrived in time for tea* or *on time for tea*?

5   Which is correct: *in ancient times* or *in ancient time*?

web·site ⚬ /'websaɪt/ *noun*
a place connected to the Internet, where a company or an organization, or an individual person, puts information: *I found this information **on their website**.* ◊ *For current prices please **visit our website**.*—picture ➩ PAGE R5

web·zine /'webziːn/ *noun* a magazine published on the Internet, not on paper

wed /wed/ *verb* (**wed·ded**, **wed·ded**) or (**wed**, **wed**) (not used in the progressive tenses) (*old-fashioned* or used in newspapers) to marry: [V] *The couple plan to wed next summer.* ◊ [VN] *Rock star to wed top model* (= in a newspaper HEADLINE).

we'd /wiːd; wid/ *short form* **1** we had **2** we would

wed·ded /'wedɪd/ *adj.* **1** ~ **to sth** (*formal*) if you are **wedded** to sth, you like or support it so much that you are not willing to give it up: *She's wedded to her job.* **2** [usually before noun] ~ (**to sb**) (*old-fashioned* or *formal*) legally married: *your **lawfully wedded** husband* ◊ *to live together in **wedded bliss*** **3** [not before noun] ~ (**to sth**) (*formal* or *literary*) combined or united with sth

wed·ding ⚬ /'wedɪŋ/ *noun*
a marriage ceremony, and the meal or party that usually follows it: *a **wedding present*** ◊ *a **wedding ceremony/ reception*** ◊ *Have you been invited to their **wedding**?* ◊ *She looked beautiful on her **wedding day**.* ◊ *All her friends could hear **wedding bells*** (= they thought she would soon get married).—see also DIAMOND WEDDING, GOLDEN WEDDING, SHOTGUN WEDDING, SILVER WEDDING, WHITE WEDDING

'wedding anniversary *noun* the celebration every year of the date when two people were married: *Today's our wedding anniversary.*

'wedding band *noun* a wedding ring in the form of a plain band, usually of gold—picture ➩ JEWELLERY

6 How could you describe someone who is old-fashioned in their way of thinking? _____

7 To encourage someone to hurry, you can say *there's no time to* _____.

8 Which is correct: *This is the first time I am in London* or *I have been to London*?

D Vocabulary building

19.5 Look at the *Vocabulary building* note at **laugh** and replace the verb in these sentences.

1 He *laughed* to himself as he remembered the funny story she'd told him. _____

2 There's no need for you to *laugh*. You sometimes make mistakes, too. _____

3 The old woman *laughed* horribly, like a witch in a children's story. _____

4 When the teacher asked them what they were doing, the girls *laughed* nervously. _____

5 'I don't believe it!' he *laughed*. That's the funniest thing I've seen in my life! _____

E Word families

19.6 Look at the *Word family* boxes for these words and fill the chart with the other members of their families.

noun	verb	adjective
		true
	rely	
		stable
ally		
	accuse	
	divide	

F Prefixes and suffixes

19.7 Complete these sentences using the prefixes and suffixes in the box.

non-   anti-   -ish   re-   ex-   mid-   self-   -sized

1 I should have finished the project by _____-January.

2 The cafe serves only _____-alcoholic drinks.

3 A group of _____-globalization protesters were demonstrating outside the building.

4 I bumped into my _____-boss at the conference.

5 We had to _____submit our application after the original application was lost.

6 There was a green_____ substance floating on the surface of the water.

7 The oven has a _____-cleaning mechanism.

8 Please supply a passport-_____ photograph of yourself.

G Language study terms

19.8 Arrange these words in categories.

comma   preposition   slang   syllable   determiner   suffix   apostrophe   prefix
semicolon   pronoun   dialect   ironic

parts of speech	*punctuation marks*	*parts of a word*	*register*
_____	_____	_____	_____
_____	_____	_____	_____
_____	_____	_____	_____

20 Arts words

A People in the arts

20.1 Complete these short definitions using words from the list of Arts words.

1   An art _____ expresses opinions about paintings, sculptures, etc.
2   A _____ writes novels.
3   An art _____ buys works of art, often as a way of investing money.
4   A _____ writes music, especially classical music.
5   A _____ stands in front of an orchestra and directs its performance.
6   An _____ designs buildings.
7   A _____ is in charge of the works of art in a museum.
8   An art _____ buys and sells pieces of art.
9   A _____ designs and arranges the movements in dances.
10 A _____ writes poems.
11 A _____ prepares and prints books and makes them available to the public.
12 A _____ makes sculptures.

B Prepositions

20.2 Circle the correct preposition in the following sentences. Use the information in your dictionary to help you.

1   The poem is attributed **on / to / by** Shakespeare.
2   The book was produced to coincide **with / for / on** an exhibition at the National Gallery.
3   She conceived **of / on / by** the building as a tower of steel and glass.
4   Brazilian culture is distinct **of / against / from** the rest of Latin American culture.
5   She incorporated the story **onto / into / with** a later novel.
6   The work was inspired **by / from / of** Japanese theatre.
7   We performed the piece as a tribute **at / towards / to** Miles Davis.

C Stress

20.3 Underline the stressed syllable in each of these Arts words and their derivatives.

architect	architecture	architectural	narrative	narrator	narration
choreography	choreographer	choreographic	orchestra	orchestral	orchestration
compose	composer	composition	poet	poetry	poetic

D Art forms

20.4 Put the words in the box into columns, depending on whether they are connected with literature, the performing arts (music, dance, drama, etc.), or the visual arts (painting, sculpture, etc.).

narrator   ballet   biography   canvas   fiction   installation   watercolour   abstract
opera   portrait   prose   quartet   solo   sonnet   symphony

literature	*performing arts*	*visual arts*
_____	_____	_____
_____	_____	_____
_____	_____	_____
_____	_____	_____
_____	_____	

21 Science words

A Scientific and technical fields

21.1 Complete these short definitions using words from the list of Science words.

1 the science or practice of farming: _____

2 the technique of producing exact copies of animals or plants: _____

3 the protection of the natural environment: _____

4 the study or use of computers: _____

5 the study of how characteristics are passed between generations: _____

6 the study of the earth, its rocks and soil: _____

7 the science of collecting and analysing information using numbers: _____

21.2 Arrange these words in categories according to which field of science they are used in.

> axis binary electron embryo equation fraction galaxy ion laser
> mammal mutation orbit organism radiation satellite solar

biology	*physics*	*astronomy*	*mathematics*
_____	_____	_____	_____
_____	_____	_____	_____
_____	_____	_____	_____
_____	_____	_____	_____

B Chemical elements

21.3 Find six chemical elements in the Science list and use the information given in your dictionary to help you to complete the table below.

name of element	*scientific symbol*	*information*
_____gold_____	Au	used for making coins, jewellery, decorative objects, etc.
_____	_____	_____
_____	_____	_____
_____	_____	_____
_____	_____	_____
_____	_____	_____

C Talking about scientific results

21.4 Complete each sentence with a word from the box.

> scattered findings long-term widespread isolated phenomena random

1 The problem is more _____ than we originally thought.

2 Cases like this are _____ over a large area.

3 We have so far discovered only a few _____ cases.

4 I'm sure you'll be very interested to read about our _____ .

5 The distribution amongst the population appears to be _____ .

6 _____ like this are rarely seen outside the laboratory.

7 We know very little about the _____ effects.

22 Business and finance words

A People in the world of business

22.1 Complete these short definitions using words from the Business and finance word list.

1 An _____ keeps the financial records of a business.
2 A market _____ gives opinions about the future profits of industries.
3 An _____ examines the financial records of companies.
4 A _____ has an important job at a financial institution.
5 An insurance _____ helps people to buy insurance.
6 A building _____ is employed by other companies to do building work.
7 An _____ studies how societies organize their money and industries.
8 An _____ deals with all the telephone calls that are made to an organization.
9 A clothes _____ runs a business that sell clothes to the public.
10 A bond _____ buys and sells bonds on a stock exchange.

B Related words

22.2 Match a word on the left with a related word on the right.

asset	borrower
boom	debtor
creditor	deficit
gross	liability
landlord	net/nett
lender	recession
purchaser	seller
surplus	tenant

C Prepositions

22.3 Circle the correct preposition in the following sentences.

1 What is the next item **by** / **in** / **on** the agenda?
2 The costs have been allocated **to** / **at** / **on** the different departments.
3 To comply **at** / **by** / **with** building regulations, all rooms must have a smoke alarm.
4 The total of these figures should correspond **by** / **to** / **on** the amount owing on the account.
5 Authority to set budgets is delegated **to** / **on** / **at** departmental managers.
6 The value of the euro is dependent **on** / **of** / **to** world markets.
7 We have invoiced you **of** / **for** / **with** all purchases up to April.
8 You and your partners will be liable **for** / **of** / **to** the debts of the business.

D Word combinations

22.4 Use your dictionary to find a word that fits both sentences in each the following pairs:

1 The company has decided to cut 300 administrative _____ .

   In the past, a greater number of people were employed in unskilled manual _____ .

2 The company announced a 12% increase in gross _____ .

   Though interim _____ were down, the airline still increased its dividend.

3 We have decided to implement a new _____ on giving refunds.

   Through its monetary _____ the reserve bank seeks to influence interest rates.

4 Many _____ traders have been unable to compete with the supermarkets.

   We offer the same rates of interest to both institutional and _____ investors.

23 New words

A New ideas

23.1 Match a word from the first column with a word from the second column to form a compound.

smoking	victim
plasma	charge
fashion	gun
congestion	factor
wow	placement
product	screen

B Where do they come from?

23.2 Put these words into columns according to the area that they are connected with.

> aquaplaning   B2B   blog   boiler room   chillout   cookie   docking station   docusoap
> golden hello   MP3 player   mystery shopper   paraglider   pay-as-you-go   quad bike
> ringtone   sim card   tribute band   wakeboarding   WAP webcast

computing	*extreme sports*	*entertainment*	*business*	*telecommunications*
_____	_____	_____	_____	_____
_____	_____	_____	_____	_____
_____	_____	_____	_____	_____
_____	_____	_____	_____	_____

23.3 Where might you see...

1 a banner ad? _____
2 a director's cut? _____
3 an emoticon? _____
4 bull bars? _____
5 a news ticker? _____
6 decking? _____
7 a water cooler? _____
8 a toll plaza? _____

C New words quiz

23.4 Answer these questions.

1 Which parliament has a **first minister**?
2 What name is given to the area where the **euro** is in circulation?
3 What are the **Noughties**?
4 Where does a **barista** work?
5 Where would you arrive if you went through a **wormhole**?
6 Why would you keep a **dreamcatcher** in your bedroom?
7 What does **nanotechnology** deal with: very small objects or very large objects?
8 In which city are **Bollywood** movies made?

D Idioms

23.5 Match the idioms in the box with these sentences.

> does what it says on the tin   it's not rocket science   wake up and smell the coffee
> think out of the box   it's not over until the fat lady sings   how long have you got?

1 We need some fresh ideas here. Let's try to _____.
2 We still have a chance to win this tournament. _____.

3   This new kitchen cleaner works well. It _____.

4   I did it all by myself. After all, _____.

5   If you think somebody will do it for you, you're wrong. _____!

6   You want to know what's wrong with it? _____

E   Abbreviations

23.6   Answer these questions with words from the box.

| RSI   SAD   DVT   LOL   PDA   GPS |

1   You might get this if you don't get enough sunlight. _____

2   You might get this if you don't move around on a long flight. _____

3   This could help you to find your way when you are lost. _____

4   You might put this at the end of an email or a text message. _____

5   You might get this if you spend a lot of time at the computer. _____

6   This might help you to organize your life. _____

F   New words in the news

23.7   Match these headlines with the summaries of the articles that they accompany. There is one extra summary.

1   **Detox is the new Botox, says celeb life coach**

2   **New chick lit sensation is not just eye candy**

3   **I'd rather have bling than boyf any day, says Miss Kirstee**

4   **If you've maxed out on your store cards, chill out!**

5   **A-list luvvy checks into rehab**

6   **New superbug drug postcode lottery**

a   A writer shows that she is intelligent as well as good-looking.

b   The writer gives advice about how to deal with debt.

c   You can never wear too much jewellery, according to a fashion expert.

d   Your chances of getting a new hospital treatment depend on where you live.

e   A famous actor goes for treatment for alcoholism.

f   A healthy diet can make you look younger.

g   A female pop star talks about her ex-boyfriend.

G   Text messaging

23.8   Look at page R57 in your dictionary and try to decipher these messages.

1   **c u l8r**

2   **r u busy?**

3   **pls cn u b here b4 10**

4   **luv u 4eva**

5   **thx 4 yr help**

24 Cultural knowledge

A People

24.1 Where do these people come from? Which nouns are informal? Is there an 'official' form?

Scousers	*Liverpool*
Angelenos	_____
Aussies	_____
Brummies	_____
Geordies	_____
Glaswegians	_____
Kiwis	_____
newfies	_____
Orcadians	_____
Martians	_____

24.2 Look up the entry for each of the names and then choose the most suitable one to fill the gaps in the sentences below.

Darby and Joan	David and Goliath	Mr. Clean	Stepford wife	Valley Girl	Walter Mitty

1 He makes out he's had a fascinating career, but it's all pure fantasy, you know. He's a bit of a _____ character.

2 Tom's new girlfriend's a real _____. She doesn't need to work, and she seems to spend all her time in town buying new clothes.

3 My grandparents are so sweet! They still hold hands when they walk down the street. They're like _____.

4 The Senator likes to come over as _____, but there are rumours that not all his business dealings were completely legal.

5 Abbie never contradicts her husband or does anything without asking him first, does she? What is she, some kind of _____?

6 When the amateur team came up against the champions in the Cup, the match was described as a contest between _____.

B Places

24.3 What kind of people would you expect to find working in these places?

Silicon Valley	*software engineers*
Fleet Street	_____
Harley Street	_____
Madison Avenue	_____
Savile Row	_____
Wall Street	_____
Tin Pan Alley	_____
Whitehall	_____

24.4 These are all unofficial or informal names for places. Do they refer to the UK or the US?

the Windy City	_____
the Square Mile	_____
Blighty	_____
the Big Apple	_____
Tinseltown	_____
the Home Counties	_____

24.5 What do these pairs of places have in common?

1 Alcatraz and Fort Knox?
2 Davy Jones's locker and Atlantis?
3 Land's End and John o'Groats?

C Adjectives

24.6 These people have had their names made into adjectives. Look them up in your dictionary and write down the name from which the adjective is derived, and the occupation of the person.

Orwellian	_Orwell_	_writer_
Confucian	_____	_____
Freudian	_____	_____
Jacobean	_____	_____
Kafkaesque	_____	_____
Machiavellian	_____	_____
Rubenesque	_____	_____
Wagnerian	_____	_____

D Institutions and events

24.7 Can you match up these names of institutions and events with the activity with which they are connected?

Bollywood	education
the Dáil	popular literature
eisteddfod	politics
the Ivy League	sport
Mills and Boon	cinema
the Six Nations	music and poetry

E Products

24.8 Match these products and the names that refer to them.

Dr Martens™	ovenproof glass
Hoover™	a mechanical digger
Jacuzzi™	a strong four-wheel-drive vehicle
JCB™	a padded envelope
Jeep™	lace-up boots
Jiffy Bag™	a whirlpool bath
Pyrex™	a vacuum cleaner

25 Using the Reference section

A The world

25.1 Answer these questions using the Maps section immediately after page 1780 of the dictionary.

1 What is the name of the southernmost point on earth?
2 What is the longitude of the Greenwich meridian?
3 Is the tropic of Cancer in the northern or the southern hemisphere?
4 What happens at longitude 180°?
5 When are the two solstices?
6 Which is the largest country in South America?
7 Northern Ireland is part of Great Britain. True or false?
8 On which of the Great Lakes is Rochester, New York?
9 Which ocean lies to the west of Australia?
10 The orbit of which planet lies between Mars and Saturn?

25.2 Answer these questions using the Geographical names section on page R85.

1 A person from Denmark is called a _____.
2 The adjective relating to Iceland is _____.
3 A person from Kuwait is a _____.
4 The adjective connected to Uruguay is _____.
5 Correct this sentence: *On the plane I met two Japaneses and a Swedish.*

B Topic vocabulary

25.3 Read the Health section on pages R18–19, then decide whether these sentences are true ✓ or false ✗.

1 If you break your arm, you have to wear a crutch.
2 When you have flu, you usually have a high temperature.
3 If you've cut your finger, you'll have to have it in plaster.
4 When you need medication, the doctor will give you a prescription.

25.4 Read the Cooking section on pages R10–11, then fill the gaps in these sentences.

1 _____ the rice for about ten minutes.
2 My mother _____ wonderful cakes.
3 If I want a very quick snack in the evenings, I just pop something in the _____.
4 When the weather's warm enough, we'll be able to have a _____ in the garden.
5 My oven isn't big enough to _____ a turkey that size.

C Correspondence in English

25.5 Read the correspondence section on pages R53–5, then decide whether these statements are true ✓ or false ✗.

1 Your write your name in the top right-hand corner of a letter.
2 *Take care* is a way of ending a letter to a friend.
3 A memo should begin *Dear Sir* or *Dear Madam*.
4 In a business letter, you put the address of the person you are writing to on the left, near the top.
5 In British English, you should finish a letter *Yours faithfully* if you began *Dear Sir/Madam*, etc.
6 When you apply for a job in Britain, it is not usual to put your date of birth on your CV.

D Punctuation

25.6 Refer to the Punctuation section on pages R60–2 to help you put the correct punctuation into these sentences.

1 He called her at the office but she wasnt there
2 Do you know where she is he asked
3 Season the soup with salt pepper and paprika
4 You like tulips dont you
5 What it cost sixty five dollars
6 Have you read Jane Austens Pride and Prejudice

E Abbreviations

25.7 Answer these questions about abbreviations. There is a list of abbreviations on page R69.

1 If a recipe says '1 **tsp** vinegar, 1 **tbsp** water', what do you need more of?
2 Where would you stay on holiday, an **A & E** or a **B & B**?
3 If a letter said **fao** followed by your name, should you read it?
4 Which qualification is higher, a **BSc** or an **MSc**?
5 If you see **PTO** at the bottom of the page, what should you do?
6 Who is older, Billy-Bob **Jr** or Billy-Bob **Sr**?
7 Where might you read '**m**, 35, **GSOH**, **WLTM f** for interesting discussions'?
8 If someone says that they have a high **IQ**, what claim are they making?
9 If an electrical appliance says '**DC** only', can you plug it in?
10 Where would you go to get some cash, an **ATM** or a **BBQ**?
11 Which salary is higher, $5 000 **p.a.** or $50 **p.w.**?
12 If you are asked for **ID**, would you show your passport or your plane tickets?

F Figure as words

25.8 Look at the expressions using figures on page xii. To solve this puzzle, write the figures in the boxes and then do the sum.

The number of the form in the US on which you give details of your income	[ ]
	÷
A vehicle in which power is applied to all four wheels is a 4 x ____	[ ]
	=
	[ ]
	−
The rating for a film that can only be legally watched by adults	[ ]
	=
	[ ]
	+
The upper level of a second class degree in Britain is called a 2:____	[ ]
	=
	[ ]
	+
The lower level of this standard of degree is a 2:____	[ ]
	=
	[ ]
	÷
For 'every hour of every day' you can also say 24/____	[ ]
	=
Why is this number important for a photographer?	[ ]

25.9 Read pages R63–4, then try writing these numbers, temperatures and amounts in words:

1   3,502 _____

2   22nd _____

3   7/10 _____

4   4 1/4 _____

5   67.9 _____

6   297448 (as a telephone number) _____

7   10°C _____

8   67°F _____

9   $52 _____

10 £1.25 _____

25.10 Now look at the sections on dates and times on pages 65–66 and choose the right answer.

1   If an American writes the date 08/10/04, it means
   a 8 October, 2004.
   b 10 August, 2004.

2   If a British speaker says the time is *five past two*, it's the same as when an American says
   a *five of two.*
   b *five after two.*

3   The time 21.45 can also be expressed as
   a 9.45 p.m.
   b 9.45 a.m.

4   If today is June 27, then June 29 is
   a the day before yesterday.
   b the day after tomorrow.

G Numbers in measurements

25.11 After you have read through the section on numbers in measurements on pages R67–8, choose one of these words to fill the gaps in the sentences.

pints	miles	gallon	pounds	feet	acres

1   The baby weighed eight _____.

2   He runs six _____ every day.

3   I bought three _____ of milk.

4   The car does about 38 miles to the _____.

5   How many _____ of land do they own?

6   My bedroom is ten _____ by eight.

1 Finding your way around the dictionary

A Alphabetical order

Explain to students that the more they practise using alphabetical order to find what they are looking for, the quicker at it they will become. Demonstrate how to use alphabetical order by choosing a word, finding the first letter of the word, then going through each letter individually until you have identified the point in the dictionary where the word should be. All spaces, apostrophes, hyphens and other punctuation marks are ignored for the purposes of alphabetical order. Upper case letters (capitals) come before lower case letters.

1.1 Get students to do section **a**, then check answers as a class. For the other sections, allocate the different words to your students (by giving them a slip of paper with their word written on it) and ask them to stand up and arrange themselves in alphabetical order according to their words. Encourage them to discuss answers with each other and come to a group consensus before checking their answers with you.

KEY **a** barley, corn, maize, millet, oats, rice, rye, wheat
  b pipeline, pipe organ, pipette, piquant, pistachio, pitch, pith, pit stop
  c seep, segment, seismic, seize, seizure, select, siesta, sieve
  d ski, skid, skier, skiing, ski lift, skin diving, skinny, ski pants
  e O, o', OAP, O-Bon, o'clock, OD, odd, O level

B Finding the right page

Show students how the first word on each left-hand page of the dictionary is shown at the top of that page. Point out the word at the top of the right-hand page and ask them what they think that is (it shows which is the last word at the bottom of that page). Explain that these words are there to help them see which page the word they are looking for is on.

The following two exercises will demonstrate this further.

1.2
KEY **Segment** is the only word which is not on these pages.
1.3
KEY **Mica**, **metronome**, **micron**, **mews** and **metre** are on these pages.

C Finding the right part of speech

Write the word **reward** on the board and ask students what part of speech it is (i.e. whether it is a noun, verb, adjective, etc.). Ask them to look at the entry to find out where the information that it can be a noun or a verb is given. Point out that the first line of the entry lists all the possible parts of speech, and that each part of speech has its own section in the entry. Each part of speech section is introduced by a square symbol (■).

1.4 Students can familiarize themselves with this feature with the exercise. To vary class feedback, draw columns on the board with the headings **noun**, **verb**, **adjective**, **adverb** and **conjunction**, and ask students to tell you which of the words go in each column.

KEY **bridge**: noun, verb
  green: adjective, noun, verb
  extra: adjective, noun, adverb
  fool: noun, verb, adjective
  prior: adjective, noun
  so: adverb, conjunction, noun

1.5 Ask students to discuss the answers to this exercise in pairs *without* looking at the dictionary at first. They can then check their ideas by looking up the entries in the dictionary.

KEY 1 adjective 4 noun 7 verb 10 adverb
  2 verb 5 adjective 8 noun
  3 adjective 6 noun 9 conjunction

D Homonyms

Write the word **sow** on the board and ask students if they know how to pronounce it and what it means. Explain that there are two ways to pronounce it and two meanings. Get students to look at the two entries and tell you what the different pronunciations and meanings are. Words like this, where two or more words are written the same but are pronounced differently and have unrelated meanings, are called **homonyms**. In the dictionary they are distinguished by means of a small number immediately following the headword.

1.6 Point out the box on the right and explain that the words inside are all examples of homonyms. Go through each homonym, checking the two different pronunciations in each case. Do the first question together, asking students to check the entries for **bow** to find which one corresponds to the word in this sentence. Students can then do the rest of the questions alone. Get them to check in pairs before checking answers as a class.

KEY 1 bow¹ 5 row¹ 9 lead¹ 13 tear¹
  2 bow² 6 row¹ 10 minute¹ 14 wind¹
  3 bow² 7 lead² 11 minute² 15 wind²
  4 row² 8 lead¹ 12 tear²

E Inflected forms

Remind students that there may be slight changes in spelling, and go through the examples below. You could write the base forms on the board and invite students to tell you the irregularities in each case:

● a change from **-c** to **-ck** in some verbs: *panic, panicking, panicked*

● a doubling of the consonant for verbs and adjectives: *grin, grinning, grinned; grim, grimmer, grimmest*

● some verbs, adjectives and nouns may have a change from *-y* to *-i*: *carry, carries, carried; happy, happier, happiest; property, properties.*

Lastly, point out that if an irregular form is very different from its base form (for example *go, went, gone*), and comes at a different place in the alphabet, students will find a cross-reference there.

1.7 The exercise can be done quite quickly and without dictionaries. At class feedback stage, you could ask different students to come and write the base form on the board, and get them to check in their dictionaries if any disagreements arise.

KEY 1 jetty 3 cruel 5 fat 7 bumpy
  2 intensify 4 grab 6 fret 8 frolic

F Choosing the right meaning

Get students to look up the word **callus** and tell you how many meanings it has (just one). Now ask them to look up the word **walnut** and tell you how many meanings it has (three: a nut, the tree which produces these nuts, and the wood from the tree). Write on the board *a walnut chair* and ask students to tell you which meaning applies (number 3, the wood).

Not all senses defined in one entry are as closely related as the three meanings of **walnut**. Ask students to look up the word **calf** and tell you the two meanings (a part of a person's leg and a young cow or other animal).

1.8 Students can do the exercise alone, then check their answers in pairs before checking answers as a class. As a follow-up to this exercise, you could get students to write their own similar questions about two or three words of their own choosing. They should then give their questions to another student to answer.

KEY
1	6	5	3
2	meaning 5	6	meaning 1
3	4	7	football (soccer)
4	meaning 3	8	a speech or piece of writing, a plant

G Specialist fields

Some words have specialist meanings in addition to their meanings in everyday language. For example, words may have a particular meaning in politics, medicine or music. Get students to look at the entry for **chord** to illustrate this, pointing out where and how the specialist meanings are mentioned.

1.9 The exercise will show students more examples of specialist meanings. You could write the following specialist areas on the board in random order: *grammar, finance, law, geology, computing, physics, medicine, economy*. Ask students to look at the words in the exercise and guess which words go with which subject, but don't worry if they do not have many ideas at this stage. They can then look up the entries in the dictionary and match the words with the words on the board.

KEY
1	geology	3	medicine	5	finance	7	economics
2	law	4	computing	6	physics	8	law, grammar

H Short cuts

In order to help students find their way around longer entries there are 'short cuts', which separate the different meanings more clearly and are designed to help them find the meaning they are looking for more quickly. Show the entry for **wave** as an example.

1.10 This exercise will give students practice in using short cuts. Look at the first question together, encouraging students to look down through the short cuts to find one that fits the context of the sentence.

KEY
1	fashion		4	in music
2	of map/diagram/model		5	of shops/hotels
3	skilful		6	in tennis

I Following up cross-references

To help students make the most of the dictionary there is a network of cross-references that point out where they can find more information. For example, if there is a picture of a word in another part of the dictionary, a cross-reference in the entry will tell them. If the word or phrase that they are looking for is defined in another place in the dictionary, they will also find a cross-reference. Irregular forms which are very different from their root words have entries at their place in the alphabet with cross-references to the headword where they can find the definition.

Point out that idioms are defined at the first important word in the phrase, for example **carved in stone** can be found at **carve**, but students will find a cross-reference at **stone**.

1.11 The exercise could be done as a race. Put students into pairs and see who can find the answers in the quickest time.

KEY
1	pan		8	fly
2	raccoon		9	nitrous oxide
3	Welsh rarebit		10	gate
4	paperknife		11	man
5	political science		12	haul
6	radius		13	injunction
7	weave		14	shout

2 The parts of an entry

A Information about the headword

At the top of each entry in *OALD* students will find certain information about the headword. Ask what information they would expect to find or need to know about a word before they can use it correctly, and try to elicit some or all of the following information. They can look at entries in the dictionary if they need to.

Write the following points on the board as you elicit them, making sure students understand what is meant in each case:

● **variants** (this may be different spellings of the headword, for example at **pygmy**, or different words which mean the same, for example at **outboard motor**)

● **variety of English** (a word may only be used in British English, for example **holiday camp**. Alternative words or spellings used in other varieties, such as American English, are given too, for example **holidaymaker/vacationer** and **honour/honor**. For more practice on varieties of English, see pages 33–34.)

● **pronunciation** (a phonetic transcription is given unless the headword is made up of more than one word. In these cases the stress is marked on the headwords themselves, for example ˌholy 'orders. If the American pronunciation varies from British pronunciation, this is also shown. For more practice on pronunciation, see pages 15–16.)

● **part of speech** (this is given at each headword. If a word can have two or more parts of speech, for example **home**, they are listed at the beginning of the entry.

● **grammar** (all irregular forms are given. This may be the past forms of a verb such as **hold**, the plural of a noun such as **hippopotamus**, or the comparative/superlative forms of an adjective such as **holy**. Also shown is whether a noun is countable or uncountable, or whether a verb takes an object or not.

● **abbreviations or symbols** (for example the abbreviations for **cent** and the symbol for **magnesium**)

● **register** (this gives information on how a word is used, for example in formal or informal language. For more practice on this, see pages 31–32.)

2.1 This exercise will reinforce this information. Students can do the questions alone. When checking answers as a class, bring students' attention back to the list of points on the board, eliciting which point each answer relates to (for example, question 1 relates to variants, question 3 to register, etc.).

As a follow-up, you could ask students to write one or two questions of their own, about an entry of their own choosing. They should base their questions on the ones in the exercise in style and structure. Depending on the number of students, they can ask each other their questions or you could deal with them open class.

KEY
1 despatch
2 verb
3 formal
4 Sr
5 The American pronunciation has an r sound.
6 a bag lunch or a box lunch
7 oz
8 air conditioning or alternating current
9 air conditioning
10 Mr.
11 metric ton
12 quotation marks

B Abbreviations

2.2 There are several abbreviations used in the dictionary to give grammar or other information about words. Get students to try the crossword without looking at the dictionary, alone and then in pairs or threes to pool their knowledge. They can check their answers by looking at the list of abbreviations and grammar labels inside the front cover of *OALD*. Check answers quickly as a class to finish.

KEY

	Across		Down
2	adjective	1	symbol
4	abbreviation	3	conjunction
6	plural	4	adverb
7	past participle	5	determiner
9	somebody	6	past tense
10	something	8	pronoun

The word that is abbreviated to **prep**. is **preposition**.

C Idioms

2.3 Show students the entry for **march** and ask the following questions:

● What part of speech is this word? *(verb and noun)*

● How many main meanings does the verb have? *(four)*

● How many meanings does the noun have? *(four)*

● What is **get your marching orders** an example of? *(an idiom, found in the section marked* **IDM** *)*

● Are there any idioms using **march** as a noun? *(Yes, one – **on the march**)*

Make sure all students are aware of what idioms are, i.e. expressions that mean something different from the normal use of the words in them. Explain that idioms are normally defined at the entry for the first 'full' word that they contain, i.e. the first noun, verb, adjective or adverb. However, in the case of **get your marching orders**, the first full word is **get**, which is too common to be a useful place to list idioms.

For more practice on idioms, see page 24.

KEY

1	three	3	price	5	noun
2	two	4	adjective	6	Both are correct.

D Phrasal verbs

Refer students back to the entry for **march** and ask them where they would find the meaning of *march on*. Explain that the section marked **PHR V** includes phrasal verbs, i.e. verbs that are used with particles such as **on**, **up** and **with** to make new meanings. Some verbs are used with a large number of different particles. For an example, students can look at the number of phrasal verbs at **hold**. Establish that they are listed in alphabetical order of the particle in the **PHR V** section, starting with **hold sth** *against* **sb**, going through to **hold** *with* **sth**.

2.4 This exercise will help familiarize students with the way phrasal verbs are presented in the dictionary. For more practice on phrasal verbs, see page 25.

KEY
1 beef sth up
2 three
3 peter out
4 to speak for a long time about something that other people may find boring
5 in position
6 two

E Derivatives

2.5 Ask students to look at the entry for **laughable**, and at the end of the entry where the related adverb **laughably** is given. This section is for words that are closely related to the headword and whose meanings are easy to work out from the definition of the headword. Ask them to look at the verb **falsify** and tell you what derivative is given there.

Students can attempt the exercise without the dictionary to start with. Which entries do they think they might find the words at? After a short time alone, get them to discuss their ideas in pairs before checking in the dictionary.

KEY

1	baffle	5	epidemic *(noun)*
2	destabilize	6	green
3	deterrent	7	magenta *(adjective)*
4	drowsy	8	racketeer

F Examples

2.6 Remind students that they should always read any examples there are for any word they look up, as they give important information on using the word correctly and naturally. This exercise will illustrate this, and the exercises on page 11 give further practice with examples.

KEY

1	Blue suits you.	4	gathering dust
2	sad	5	home
3	famous buildings	6	on location

G Help

2.7 Explain that there are extra notes at certain entries to help students with common errors, especially in grammar. Get students to try the exercise without looking at the dictionary, to compare their ideas in pairs and then to look in the dictionary to check their answers.

KEY
1 Ask her what's wrong.
2 I don't want to play any more.
3 Every individual's fingerprints are totally/absolutely unique.
4 Can you please explain the problem to me?
5 I've been waiting for the bus for half an hour.
6 My new TV has an LCD screen.
7 The headmaster wanted to know what I was doing.
8 Can you suggest a good restaurant?

3 Looking at definitions

The definitions in *OALD* are written in simple language to help students understand the meanings easily, using the words from the *Oxford 3000* list of keywords. Some words, for example those that describe categories of things in the world, are very important for understanding definitions. The following activities focus on some of the most frequent words that they will read in the dictionary.

A It's a type of...

3.1 Write the phrase **an Indian summer** on the board and elicit or explain the meaning (a period of unusually warm weather in autumn). Establish that the word **Indian** actually has little to do with the meaning of the phrase and that they are going to see other phrases with the names of countries.

They should match the expressions on the left with a word or expression on the right. When they have tried this on their own, refer students to the first question and elicit the sentences *I think American football is a kind of sport* and … *is a type of sport*. They should then work in pairs, using these phrases to check their answers with each other. Finally, they can check in the dictionary for the correct answers.

KEY American football is a type of sport.
Chinese cabbage is a type of vegetable.
A French horn is a type of musical instrument.
German measles is a type of illness.
An Afghan hound is a type of dog.
A Danish pastry is a type of cake.
Turkish delight is a type of sweet/candy.

3.2 Explain to students that the words in the box are ones which are very often used in definitions. Give them a couple of minutes to look at these words, helping each other and ensuring that they know what they mean. They can then put the words into the appropriate blanks. Get them to check in pairs before going over the answers as a class, looking in the dictionary if there are answers that they disagree about.

KEY
1	container	5	machine	9	state
2	device	6	substance	10	quality
3	instrument	7	process	11	organization
4	tool	8	feeling	12	act

3.3 To do class feedback for this exercise, you could write the category headings on the board and invite students to come up and write the words into the appropriate columns. Alternatively, simply elicit the correct answers from the students, getting them to give you full sentences using *a type/kind of…*

KEY
vehicle	SUV, rickshaw
aircraft	glider, microlight
dish	haggis, tikka
cloth	satin, tweed
solid	ingot, wax
liquid	lava, venom
gas	ozone, helium

B Adjectives often used in definitions

3.4 The purpose of this exercise is to help students understand the precise meanings of the descriptions in the dictionary. First refer students to the list of nouns and briefly make sure that they know what the objects are, but avoid using any of the adjectives at this stage. They should then work in pairs to allocate adjectives to objects. During class feedback, elicit full sentences from students, using words from previous exercises, for example *satin is a type of smooth, shiny, soft cloth; cream is a smooth, pale substance*, etc.

KEY
1	thin, flat	4	smooth, pale
2	smooth, shiny, soft	5	long, round
3	small, sharp, pointed	6	rough, thick

FOLLOW-UP EXERCISE

Students now have the vocabulary and structures they need to play a defining game. Put students into pairs and give them a few nouns each, for example Student A has **coffee**, **scooter** and **jealousy** and Student B has **honesty**, **hammer** and **peacock**. Give them a few minutes alone to prepare simple definitions using the vocabulary and structures covered in these exercises. They should take it in turns to define their own words and guess each other's words.

4 Looking at examples

Explain to students that the examples in *OALD* can be useful in many different ways. Write the following points on the board, to show students what they can learn from example sentences:

- meaning (*examples help students understand more about the meaning of a word*)
- common collocates of the word (*i.e. the words with which it frequently appears: the typical subjects and objects of a verb, the adverbs and adjectives which often come up with particular verbs and nouns, etc.*)
- grammatical structures
- typical contexts

A What examples can tell you

4.1 This exercise will illustrate the above points and show students the kind of information they can get from looking at examples.

KEY
1	a	give, follow, seek, take;
	b	doctors and lawyers;
	c	a piece of advice, a word of advice
2	a	a bottle;
	b	the perfume counter;
	c	yes
3	a	a communications satellite, a rocket;
	b	a torpedo, a missile, a rocket;
	c	an appeal, enquiry, investigation or campaign, an attack or invasion, a new product, a ship or boat
4	a	cold and wind;
	b	disappointment;
	c	yes

B Figurative examples

Get students to look at the entry for **pendulum**. First, establish the meaning (a part of a clock). Then direct them to the two examples. They should notice that the examples have nothing to do with clocks. Point out the *figurative* label, which shows that the following example(s) do not refer to the literal meaning of the word and show the word being used in a different context, often to add a more dramatic quality. Can students see the connection between the literal and the figurative uses? Just as the pendulum of a clock swings from one side to another, so do opinions and trends go from one extreme to the other.

4.2 Look at the first question together and ask students to look at the entry for **infectious**. Get them to tell you why the two words are often used together (**infectious** is usually used about diseases that can pass from person to person, so it means laughter that spreads as more and more people start laughing).

Students should work in pairs to discuss the remaining questions before going through them as a class.

KEY
2	**Iron** is a hard, strong metal, so a *will of iron* shows a strong, powerful will.
3	**Mouth-watering** refers to food which looks so good you want to eat it immediately, so *mouth-watering travel brochures* would make you want to visit the places they show.
4	A **maze** is a system of paths divided by walls or hedges to make it difficult to get out of, so a *maze of corridors* in a building means it is hard to find your way around.
5	To **replay** is to play again sth that has been recorded on tape, film, etc., so *he replayed the scene in his mind* means that he thought over what had happened again.
6	To **pension sb off** is to allow or force somebody to retire, so if a car *should have been pensioned off* it means it is old or broken down and should no longer be driven.

C Collocations in examples

Get students to look up the entry for **occasion**. They will see that in the first two senses of the word there are parts of the examples that are highlighted in bold. Explain that these are common collocations – combinations of words that are very frequently used together. For more practice with collocations, see pages 28–29.

4.3 Students should be given plenty of time to complete the exercise. Before checking answers as a class, get students to check their ideas in pairs and help each other with any problems.

KEY
1	without a **murmur**	5	in the **old** days
2	set to **music**	6	to the best of my **ability**
3	have a **nice** time	7	out of **sight**
4	make a **note** of	8	**novelty** value

5 Looking at notes

In *OALD* a lot of extra information is given in special notes which help students decide which word to use, build up their vocabulary, avoid grammatical mistakes and find out more about English and the English-speaking world. (Point out that there is a list of all the entries which have notes on page R93–6 in the dictionary.) Each of the activities on these pages focuses on a different type of note.

A Which word?

The dictionary helps decide which is the correct word in cases where people often have doubts. A list of these *Which word?* notes can be found on page R93 in the dictionary.

5.1 Students should do this exercise individually. If they are having difficulty identifying where the errors are, tell them that the notes can be found at these entries: **lastly**, **long**, **interested**, **compliment**, **especially**, **say**, **used to**, **affect**.

KEY At the weekend, I **finally**/**at last** had the chance to see a play that I had been wanting to see for a **long time**. I am very **interested** in the theatre, and my friend was playing the leading role. Afterwards I met my friend and **complimented** him on his performance, **especially** his amazing calmness. He **told** me that when he first started acting he **used to** get very nervous, but now he was less **affected** by nerves.

B Vocabulary building

The notes on vocabulary building in *OALD* help students to broaden their vocabulary and to express themselves more precisely and in a more interesting way in English. It is not wrong to talk about *bad conditions* or *nice weather*, but these words are used so much that they no longer seem very powerful, so they should try to find better ways of expressing these ideas. The *Vocabulary building* notes suggest other possibilities and show them how to use them in context.

5.2 This exercise can be done in pairs. Students will find the notes that give the relevant information by looking up the word in bold type.

KEY
1	appalling	6	fashionable
2	foul	7	slices
3	horrific, fractured	8	issue
4	delicious, aroma	9	characteristic
5	beautiful	10	subjects

C Grammar notes

The *Grammar* notes in *OALD* help students to find the correct construction and to avoid common errors.

5.3 This exercise can be done in pairs. The relevant *Grammar* notes can be found at the entry for the first word in each line.

KEY
1 We very much enjoy playing tennis *or* We enjoy playing tennis very much.
2 I had to wait half an hour in the queue.
3 We used to go to Wales for our holidays.
4 I love my house very much but I don't spend much time there.
5 Henry's was the old one *or* The old one was Henry's.

5.4 Students will find the notes that give the relevant information by looking up the word in bold type.

KEY   1 knew   2 on, at   3 is   4 ourselves

6 Looking at illustrations

There are various types of illustration in *OALD*, serving a variety of purposes. In the main A – Z section of the dictionary, some illustrations show the meaning of a word in a more direct way than a definition is sometimes able to do; others group together words that have similar meanings or from a particular topic or field. In addition, the Reference section brings together material that can be exploited for vocabulary study purposes. These exercises are designed to familiarize students with the illustrations in the dictionary and help them get the most out of this valuable resource.

A Objects from around the world

6.1 Get students to look at the illustration near the entry for **dreamcatcher** and ask what they think it is and where it is from. Then get them to look at the definition to see if they were right. They should then try the exercise without dictionaries, using them to check their answers when they have finished. To reinforce pronunciation and meanings of the new vocabulary they can then work in pairs, with books closed, asking each other *What's an ankh? It's a...; It's for...*

KEY
1	boomerang	a	weapon	Australia
2	ankh	e	symbol of life/ piece of jewellery	Egypt
3	pak choi	c	vegetable/cabbage	China
4	cheongsam	d	dress/piece of clothing	China/ Indonesia
5	bonsai	b	tree	Japan
6	salwar kameez	f	a suit of clothes	South Asia

B Adjectives

6.2 **Cracked** and **broken** have separate entries as adjectives, but the entry for **chipped** is at the verb **chip**. When students have completed the exercise, ask them to brainstorm other words to do with damage, e.g. **stained**, **marked**, **scratched**, **torn**, **frayed**, **rotten**, **bent**, **ripped**, **singed**, **charred**, **burnt**.

KEY   1 broken   2 chipped   3 cracked

6.3 When students have filled the gaps, they can check their answers with the illustration in the dictionary. To practise this vocabulary, ask each student to draw a diagram or pattern on a blank sheet of paper, using different kinds of line. They must then describe this to a partner who, without seeing the original, should try to draw what is described. Students can then compare drawings to check understanding. A similar activity can be done with the illustration at **solid**.

KEY
1	straight	4	zigzag	7	vertical
2	curved	5	dotted	8	horizontal
3	wavy / wiggly	6	parallel	9	diagonal

C Verbs

The differences between **squeeze**, **squash** and **crush** are not always easy to grasp. Illustrations make the task of understanding meaning easier.

6.4 These sentences are all examples at the entries for **squeeze**, **crush**, **squash** and **press**, so students should look in these entries to check their answers.

KEY   1 press   2 squeeze   3 squashed   4 crushed

6.5 What else can you **squeeze**, **crush**, **squash** or **press**? Students should use their dictionaries to extend their knowledge of meanings and collocations associated with these verbs.

KEY   1 press   2 squeezed   3 squash   4 crushed

6.6 Performing the actions will help students to differentiate between these similar words. As a follow-up to this exercise, students should work in groups of five or six. Each student in turn performs an action and asks the others to say what they are doing. See also the illustrations at **arm**, **cross-legged**, **leapfrog**, **shrug**.

KEY
1	squatting	3	crouching	5	on your hands and knees
2	crawling	4	kneeling		

D Topic vocabulary

6.7 This exercise can be done by brainstorming as a class before looking at the illustrations on pages R10–11 of the dictionary.

6.8 Before doing this exercise you can have a brainstorming session as for the previous exercise, but with musical instruments. Then look at the Musical instruments section (pages R6–7 of the dictionary).

Ask students to use their dictionaries to find out what name is given to players of the instruments listed. Note that if no special name for the player is given in the dictionary, the form with **player** is used (e.g. **horn player**).

KEY violin, violinist; guitar, guitarist; piano, pianist; oboe, oboist; trumpet, trumpeter; harp, harpist; clarinet, clarinettist; cello, cellist; horn, horn player; drum, drummer; flute, flautist (*NAmE* flutist); bass, bassist *or* bass player

7 Pronunciation

A Phonetic transcriptions

OALD helps learners to pronounce English words correctly by showing the pronunciation of all the words that are defined in it. All entries which are single words have the transcription after the headword, for example at the entry for **chime**. Show students that the symbols used in the transcriptions are listed on pages R118–9 of the dictionary, and that they also appear along the bottom of the page, together with a simple word to help them remember which sound each one stands for. They should use this information to complete the first two exercises below.

7.1 Ask students to look at the bottom of the dictionary pages and find the two symbols /tʃ/ and /k/, and to tell you how they are pronounced. You could then ask them to try the exercise without the dictionary first, and then to check their answers by looking up the words. Finish with class feedback, getting students to repeat the words to reinforce the correct pronunciation.

KEY /tʃ/: chirp, chin, chipmunk, chisel, cello
/k/: chiropodist, choir, chord, Celtic, character

7.2 Put students into pairs (Student A and Student B) and give them a short time to work out what the pronunciation of the words might be, saying the words to each other and without looking in the dictionary. Then give them time on their own to refer to their dictionaries. Student A should look up the words in the first column and Student B should look up the words in the second column, making a note of the pronunciation as they check the words. Then in pairs again they should speak their words to each other and see if the pronunciation is the same or different. Check the answers as a class to finish.

KEY **Pronounced the same:** wry/rye; rein/reign; knot/not; phew/few; pallet/palate
Pronounced differently: ail/aisle; known/none; pull/pool

7.3 Again, students will benefit from a short time looking at the words in pairs to see if they know or can guess which is the silent consonant in each case. They can then check their guesses in the dictionary. Rather than getting all students to look up all the words, you could go around the class allocating one word to each student so that they only have to look up one. Students should tell each other what they have discovered before a final class feedback.

KEY gnome   honorary   freight
wrathful   thumbnail   indebted
honeycomb castle   palmtop
receipt   pseudonym

7.4 Students may be able to do this exercise without dictionaries. Put them into pairs to see if they can work out the pronunciation of each word, then discuss answers as a class.

KEY Only one: the *g* is pronounced /dʒ/ in all six words.

7.5 To vary feedback, you could ask students to come up to the board to write the words in the appropriate columns.

KEY

/g/	/f/	not pronounced
ghetto	cough	thorough
gherkin	tough	though
ghost	laughter	bough

7.6 Now students have had a bit of practice with phonetic transcriptions, they should be able to read these words. At feedback, drill the words to ensure that students have read the transcriptions correctly, and point out the way stress is marked on words of more than one syllable.

KEY

1	shower	6	gesture
2	email	7	halve
3	tutor	8	thinking
4	guest (*also* guessed)	9	vicious
5	visual	10	nightmare

7.7 First, put students into pairs to read the phonetic transcriptions. Do they know any words that are pronounced like that, or can they guess how such a word might be spelt? Go through the pronunciations as a class and elicit any ideas they may have, but don't worry if they don't find all the answers.

KEY

1	colonel, kernel	6	ewe, U, yew, you
2	desert, dessert	7	wail, whale
3	core, corps, cor	8	dear, deer
4	floury, flowery	9	toe, tow
5	cent, scent, sent	10	sew, so, sow

7.8 Ask students what they think is the most common sound in English. Tell them it is the sound /ə/ (sometimes called **schwa**), checking that everyone knows what the sound is and getting a couple of example words that contain this sound (for example **again** and **sister**). Students can then work in pairs to do this exercise. Check pronunciation of all words during class feedback, drawing students' attention to the sound /ə/.

KEY **Cramped** and **undeterred** do not contain the sound /ə/.

B Stress

Multi-word headwords, like **chief of staff**, which are made up of more than one word, are marked to show where the stress falls. Refer students to the entry and point out the marks ' and ˌ. Demonstrate that the ' mark shows where the main stress falls and the ˌ mark indicates secondary stress (some stress, but less strong than the main stress). Get students to use this information to tell you how **chief of staff** is pronounced.

7.9 Students can work in pairs to say the words to each other and say where they think the main stress is in each case. They can then use their dictionaries to check their ideas before class feedback.

KEY

mixed a<u>bi</u>lity	<u>eye</u>-catching
half-<u>time</u>	<u>ba</u>lance sheet
far-<u>sigh</u>tedness	<u>sign</u> language

7.10 Explain that the same stress marks are used within the phonetic transcription to show students which part of a word is stressed, for example look at **portable** (stress is on the first syllable) and **potato** (stress is on the middle syllable).

Students can work in pairs to begin with. Ask them to try saying the words to each other to see where the stress falls. They can then check their ideas in the dictionary before class feedback.

KEY **Conclude**, **eliminate**, **phenomenon** and **philosophy** are not stressed on the first syllable.

7.11 The last two exercises focus on shifting stress, where the stress changes in different parts of speech.

KEY
1	po**li**tics	po**li**tical	poli**ti**cian
2	**pho**tograph	pho**to**grapher	photo**gra**phic
3	con**spire**	con**spi**racy	conspira**to**rial
4	in**form**	in**for**mative	infor**ma**tion
5	de**port**	depor**tee**	depor**ta**tion
6	**cele**brate	**cele**bratory	cele**bra**tion
7	**edu**cate	edu**ca**tion	edu**ca**tional
8	pro**fess**ion	pro**fess**ional	pro**fess**ionalism

7.12 During or after class feedback you could get students to read the sentences aloud, paying attention to the words in bold and placing stress in the appropriate place.

KEY
1	record	5	deserted.	9	conflict
2	recorded	6	desert	10	conflicting.
3	object	7	progress.	11	perfect
4	object	8	progressing	12	perfect

8 Spelling

A Finding the spelling

When looking for a words whose spelling is unknown, students should write down any letters of the word that they do know. If they have the first two or three, it should not be too difficult to find the word. They should try to guess any missing letters, thinking about whether they are vowels or consonants and which letters can be used in that position. Playing hangman will help to refine this skill. Choose a word from the dictionary that you think your students will not know. When they have guessed a letter correctly, elicit what letters could go on either side of it. Continue like this until the word is complete.

8.1 This exercise is designed to help students find a word in the dictionary when they do not know the exact spelling. They will also need to consider the context, and therefore the meaning, in order to find the correct word in the dictionary.

KEY
1	doldrums	3	ignoramus	5	swingeing
2	frump	4	blasé	6	mynah

B Spelling variations

8.2 Write **gaol** and **jail** on the board. Elicit the pronunciation and meaning of both and establish that the only difference is the spelling. Words like this are called **homophones**. Get learners to look up both words in *OALD* to see how each is presented. Establish which is the most usual spelling (**jail**). Now students try the exercise using the dictionary.

KEY
1	chamomile	4	hairdryer	7	benefited
2	strait-laced	5	focusing	8	medieval
3	eyeing	6	nosy		

C British and American spellings

In *OALD*, words are defined under their British spelling, and the American spelling is also shown after the headword. The American spelling will also be found at its normal place in the dictionary, unless it is very close, with a cross-reference to the British spelling. This can be demonstrated with reference to the entry **plough / plow**.

8.3 Start by eliciting some differences between British and American spelling. In this exercise, students should complete the first two columns. Then they complete the third column with other words that follow the same pattern, checking their answers in the dictionary.

KEY
British	American	Other examples
colour	color	humour / humor, favour / favor
litre	liter	centre / center, theatre / theater
defence	**defense**	licence / license (*noun*), offence / offense
travelling	traveling	cancelling / canceling, pedalling / pedaling

fulfil	**fulfill**	skilful / skillful, appal / appall
analyse	analyze	paralyse / paralyze, breathalyse / breathalyze
catalogue	catalog	dialogue / dialog, analogue / analog

D Silent letters

Elicit some English words with silent letters (for example **half**, **lamb**, **although**). Ask how many letters in the alphabet they think can be silent (all of them except *j*, *o*, *v* and *y*).

Learners should work in pairs using the dictionary to try to complete the words in as short a time as possible.

8.4
KEY
1	sub**t**le	3	diaphra**g**m	5	sa**pp**hire	7	qual**m**s
2	indi**c**ted	4	ve**h**emently	6	as**th**ma	8	solem**n**

E Non-standard spellings

Sometimes a different, non-standard spelling is used to represent the way people actually speak. You often find these words in songs, very informal writing and dialogue to show that somebody speaks in a particular way. They should only be used in these situations.

Write on the board some song titles including non-standard spellings that students are likely to be familiar with, for example *U gotta let go, Gotta get her outta my head, Crazy bout ya, Gangsta lovin', Every kinda people*. Elicit 'translations' into standard English spelling.

8.5 Students read the sentences written in non-standard spelling and write the words in bold in standard spelling. All of these non-standard spellings can be found in *OALD*. After they have completed the exercise they may be able to provide you with song titles with non-standard spellings.

KEY
1	what	4	because	7	your	10	give me
2	going to	5	want to	8	them		
3	I'm not	6	don't know	9	love		

F Sounds people make

Elicit what sounds people make in comics, etc. when they hurt themselves (**ouch**), sneeze (**ahchoo**), etc. These are conventionalized spellings for sounds which are not really words, but which people make under particular circumstances.

8.6 Students do the exercise individually, making a note of the pronunciation as they look up the words in *OALD*. They should then practise saying the sentences to each other in pairs.

You could follow this up by asking them to write six new sentences using the words in the exercise which were not chosen (**psst, ahem, phew, tut, sh, uh-oh**), again paying attention to the pronunciation so that they can practise saying them to each other.

KEY
1	Ugh	3	Um	5	Brrr
2	Aha!	4	Hmm	6	Oi

G First letters

Learners can do research with the dictionary to help them raise awareness of spelling patterns. This in turn will help them use the dictionary more effectively to look up words they do not know how to spell.

8.7 For this exercise, students look at the table and guess the answers with a partner, trying to produce sample words. When they have finished this, they should check in the dictionary. Monitor how they are doing this and guide them towards more efficient methods if necessary.

After you have checked answers you could ask them if the letter strings could be used in any other positions in words (but this is more difficult to check in the dictionary).

9 Looking at verbs

A Irregular verbs

There is information about the past tense and past participle of irregular verbs in the Reference section of *OALD* (pages R26–8). This information (along with any pronunciation that is different) can also be found at the individual entries for irregular verbs. Information is also given at the entry if the verb changes its spelling in the past tense or in the present participle, for example by doubling a consonant. Demonstrate this by looking at the entry for **bet**: **bet**, **betting**, **bet**, **bet**.

9.1
KEY
1	rung	5	spent
2	wore	6	shone
3	stung, swelled	7	risen
4	froze	8	woke

B Spelling irregularities

9.2
KEY
1 travelled (traveled *in N American English*)
2 lying
3 hopped
4 panicked
5 referred
6 dying

C Structures with verbs

In order to use verbs in grammatically correct constructions, it is important to look at the information in the entries about the structures in which they appear. Before doing the exercises, students should first read pages R36–8 of their dictionaries on verb patterns. Note that structures are often shown by means of examples as well as codes.

9.3 This exercise looks at verbs with and without objects (those with codes **V**, **V+adv./prep.**, **VN**, **VNN**).

KEY
1	no	4	no	7	yes	10	yes
2	yes	5	no	8	yes	11	yes
3	yes	6	yes	9	yes	12	yes

9.4 This exercise looks at verbs with infinitives or –*ing* forms (**V-ing**, **Vtoinf**).

KEY
1	building	4	changing	7	seeing	10	to tell
2	to arrive	5	to try	8	going		
3	taking	6	eating	9	to see		

9.5 This exercise focuses on information about structures following verbs given in bold in the verb entries. Tell students to look up **disconnect**. The pattern **disconnect sth (from sth)** tells you that you can say, for example: *I disconnected the power* or *I disconnected the cooker from the mains*.

KEY
1	from, of	3	with	5	from
2	from, to	4	with, about		

D Extra information about verbs

Students will find other pieces of useful information about the grammar of verbs in the entries, either at the beginning of the entry or numbered sense, or after the symbol **HELP**.

9.6
KEY
1	pain	3	pardon	5	bother
2	bulge	4	handicap	6	begrudge

E Verb phrases

These exercises look at verb phrases. Many verb phrases which are less fixed than idioms are given in the form of examples, sometimes highlighted with bold type to show that they are strong collocations. As an example, point out the phrase *get the message* at sense 24 of **get**.

9.7 This exercise should be done in pairs. The answers to these can all be found in examples at the entry **get**.

KEY
1	got dressed	3	got married	5	got far
2	got a shock	4	got talking		

9.8 This exercise looks at verb phrases using nouns, which are sometimes used in place of the related verb. For example, *have a try* has a similar meaning to the verb **try**. This is shown in an example at **try** (*noun*).

Students should work on their own, then compare answers. The answers to these can all be found in examples at the entries for the nouns.

KEY
1	made	3	gave	5	do
2	have	4	go	6	took

10 Looking at nouns

A The plural of nouns

Elicit from students the normal way to make plural nouns in English, i.e. by adding –s or –es. Can they think of any plural nouns that are not formed in this way (e.g. **sheep** and **children**)? Explain that any exceptions to the rule are shown in the dictionary at the top of the entry. Sometimes the whole plural form is given (as in entries for **sheep** and **children**), but sometimes only the ending changes (look at the entry for **party**).

10.1 After time alone looking up any words they don't know, ask students to come and write the plural forms on the board.

KEY
thesis, theses	bacterium, bacteria
aircraft, aircraft	salmon, salmon
crony, cronies	embryo, embryos
sister-in-law, sisters-in-law	housewife, housewives
gateau, gateaux	fungus, fungi
criterion, criteria	bottle opener, bottle openers
deer, deer	appendix, appendices

10.2 At feedback, demonstrate the fact that these nouns are always plural by looking at the examples at the entries (they all have *a pair of…*).

KEY They are always plural.

B Singular or plural

10.3 Get students to try this exercise without looking in the dictionary; any disagreements during feedback can be cleared up by looking up problematic words.

KEY 1 – 3 Both forms are possible, but the plural form is mostly used in technical English.
4 **is. Spaghetti** is uncountable in English.
5 **are. Bacteria** is the plural of **bacterium**.

10.4 Allocate one word to each student in the class. Get students to look up their word in the dictionary to find out whether it is singular or plural, as well as other information such as meaning, etc. Get students to divide themselves into two groups, one for the plural nouns and one for the singular ones.

Check their answers as a class, writing the words on the board in two columns according to whether they are singular or plural.

KEY goods, odds, valuables, basics

C Singular or plural verb

Explain to students that some nouns are only singular and cannot be used in the plural. Refer them to the entry for **onset** and point out the [sing.] label which shows this. Other nouns, for example **individuality**, are uncountable (indicated by the symbol [U]), which also means that they have no plural form. Get students to read page R42–3 in *OALD* about countable, uncountable, plural and singular nouns, which will help them with the following exercises.

10.5 Again, students can try this exercise without the dictionary to begin with. After some time alone, get them to check their ideas in pairs. Then they need only look up the words they are still unsure of. Go through answers as a class.

KEY 1   **are**

2 – 8 Both are possible in British English; only the singular is possible in American English.

D Countable and uncountable

Explain to students that words with several meanings may be used differently in different senses. For example, the names of materials are usually uncountable. Get students to look up the entry for silver and ask them the following questions:

- how many meanings does **silver** have? (*five*)
- when it refers to the metal, is it countable or uncountable? (*uncountable*)
- and coins? (*uncountable*)
- in what meaning can **silver** be used as a countable noun (*when it means 'a silver medal'*)
- can you say 'He won two silvers at the Olympic Games'? (*yes*)

10.6 This exercise will give students practice with nouns that can be countable and uncountable. They should work in pairs before class feedback.

KEY 1 The chemical element **tin** is uncountable. A **tin** is a metal container for packaging food and drink.

2 The metal **bronze** is uncountable. A **bronze** is a work of art made out of bronze, or a bronze medal.

3 **Pottery**, meaning pots, dishes etc., is uncountable. A **pottery** is a place where pots, etc. are made.

4 **Properties** can mean the possessions that are owned by somebody, or the characteristics that something has.

5 **Paper** as a material for writing on and as a wall covering are uncountable.

10.7 When you go through these answers, get students to tell you why each sentence is correct or not, to check that they have interpreted the information in the dictionary correctly.

KEY 1 no – **advice** is uncountable (*It was very useful advice.*)

2 yes

3 no – **information** is uncountable (*more information*)

4 no – **furniture** is uncountable (*The furniture is...*)

5 no – **cutlery** is uncountable (*a set of cutlery*)

E Nouns with prepositions

Explain to students that the dictionary entries will also tell them which structures can be used with nouns. This information is given before the definition in bold and is important as it will help them use words correctly in a sentence.

Get them to look at the first two meanings at the entry for **guide** and to tell you what structure is often used with this word, i.e. the preposition **to** followed by another noun. Look at the examples given in the entry.

10.8 Students can try to complete the exercise without looking in the dictionary, looking up the ones they are not sure of.

KEY 1 at   3 for   5 for

2 for   4 to   6 on

F One of...

10.9 Ask students to look at the words after **of** in this exercise. Are they countable or uncountable? Establish that they are usually uncountable, but are made up of individual elements, for example **rain** is uncountable but you can say *a drop of rain* or *several drops of rain*.

Students will find that the necessary information for this exercise is given at both nouns in each phrase, often in the examples sections.

KEY 1 grain   3 grain   5 piece   7 flake

2 piece   4 blade   6 speck

G A certain amount of...

10.10 The nouns in the box are all used to talk about a small amount of something.

KEY 1 inch   4 chink   7 gust

2 flash   5 shred   8 glimmer

3 round   6 breath   9 spot

H Adjectives as nouns

10.11 At class feedback, elicit the fact that if **the** is used, there is no –*s* on the noun (*the injured, the poor*, etc.). If it is used without **the**, the noun is plural (*whites, blonds*, etc.).

KEY 1 *The injured...*   4 *Blonds...*

2 correct   5 *... a bunch of crazies.*

3 *... the poor.*   6 correct

11 Looking at adjectives

A Adjectives in comparisons

Write the following on the board:

The Nile is a very _____ river. It is _____ than the Amazon. It is the _____ river in the world.

Ask students to complete the sentences with different forms of **long** (i.e. **long, longer** and **longest**). For adjectives of one syllable, the comparative and superlative forms are formed by adding –*er* and –*est*. Refer students to the entry for **long** so they can see how this information is given in the dictionary.

Ask students how to form the comparative and superlative of longer adjectives of three or more syllables (i.e. by using **more** and **most**). Ask them to complete the following sentences with a suitable phrase including a long adjective in the comparative or superlative:

Read this story – it's _____. (e.g. *more interesting*) *It's _____ house on this street.* (e.g. *the most beautiful; the most expensive*)

Explain that adjectives of two syllables can either be like **long**, especially if they end in –*er*, –*y* or –*ly*; others are like **interesting**. Students should refer to the dictionary if they are unsure.

11.1 Sometimes there are slight changes in the spelling of comparative and superlative forms, and a few adjectives have completely irregular forms. This exercise focuses on some of these. Students can try to complete it without looking at the dictionary, then check in the dictionary any adjectives that they are unsure of.

KEY   nice, nicer, nicest   foggy, foggier, foggiest

tidy, tidier, tidiest   lucky, luckier, luckiest

hot, hotter, hottest   good, better, best

cruel, crueller, cruellest   bad, worse, worst

dense, denser, densest   far, farther, farthest *or* further, furthest

B Adjectives with nouns

Get students to read the information on page R47 of their dictionaries about adjectives that cannot be used before a noun and those that are only used before nouns before doing the following exercises.

11.2 Allocate one word to each student in the class and give them a minute or two to check the meaning, pronunciation, etc. of their word in the dictionary. They should then move around the class and find a partner so that each adjective is matched with a noun.

Check answers as a class, making sure students have paired up correctly, and checking meaning, etc. as you go. Point out that they will usually find these common collocations of adjective + noun in the examples section of entries in the dictionary.

KEY

wavy hair	a mixed-up teenager
a sharp distinction	high finance
a steady boyfriend	chubby cheeks
a rhetorical question	a secluded beach
solid gold	a devastating cyclone

11.3 This exercise focuses on whether certain adjectives should come before or after the noun. Do the first question as a class, getting students to look up the entry for **asleep** and pointing out the [not before noun] label.

Give students time alone to complete the exercise, then ask them to check in pairs before class feedback.

KEY
1 no – *the sleeping guard*
2 no – *What is the chief problem?*
3 yes
4 yes
5 no – *It's just an interim solution.*
6 no – *the frightened children*
7 yes
8 no – *a lone tree*

C Adjectives with prepositions

Explain that some adjectives are followed by prepositions in some senses. Refer students to the entry for **exempt** to complete the following sentence as an example:

Pensioners are exempt _____ prescription charges.

11.4 Students can try to fill in the gaps without the dictionary to begin with, using it to check only answers they are unsure of.

KEY

1	about	3	about	5	to	7	of
2	with	4	at	6	about	8	to

D Adjectives with verbs

Write the following on the board and ask students to complete the sentences using the verb in brackets in an appropriate form:

It would be useful _____ how that works. (know)
This tool is useful _____ small repairs around the house. (do)

They can refer to the entry for **useful** to find the answers, i.e. *to know* and *for doing*.

12 Idioms

Idioms are expressions that have special meanings. Knowing the meanings of the individual words in the phrases may not help to understand the whole expression, so they are explained separately in *OALD*. For details of where in the entries to find idioms, see page R49 in the dictionary. Students should read this section (perhaps as homework) before tackling the exercises.

The idioms in *OALD* range from sayings and proverbs which may have been in the language for centuries, through colourful comparisons and similes, to expressions that are used very commonly in everyday situations.

A Sayings

12.1 Sayings are idioms which people use to comment on what they see as universal truths about human life. Students should try to complete these sayings before looking at the dictionary, using their knowledge of sayings in their own language, where appropriate, as well as their interpretation of the meaning. They should then check their answers in

pairs using the dictionary (they may need help with finding the idioms – remind them to look at the first 'full' word and make use of cross-references). As you are discussing the answers as a class, ask whether sayings with similar meanings exist in the students' own language(s).

KEY

1	son	4	go	7	money	10	means
2	one	5	served	8	way		
3	boys	6	perfect	9	cover		

12.2 Many sayings are so well known that people often leave off the second half of the sentence. The beginnings of these idioms can all be used on their own as well as in their full versions. When students have matched the beginnings with the ends, they should check their answers in the dictionary.

KEY

1	b	4	j	7	c	10	f
2	d	5	e	8	i		
3	g	6	h	9	a		

B Expressions used in particular circumstances

12.3 Students should work in pairs to choose the correct expression using their dictionaries. Again, they may need help with finding the idioms in the dictionary.

KEY
1 Don't ask me!
2 You're welcome!
3 Don't bet on it!
4 Do me a favour!
5 In your dreams!
6 I told you so!
7 That's the idea!
8 How come?
9 Let's not even go there!
10 Here we go!
11 How does that grab you?

13 Phrasal verbs

Explain to students that in *OALD* phrasal verbs are explained separately from the main meanings of the verbs. For more information on phrasal verbs, see pages R40–1 in the dictionary.

A New phrasal verbs

13.1 Phrasal verbs are a rich area of vocabulary change in English, and new combinations of verbs with particles are being created all the time. This exercise focuses on a few of them. Students should look up the relevant verb in each case to find the phrasal verbs in question.

KEY
1 beat yourself up   4 fed into   7 cut ... up
2 click through   5 zoned out   8 scope out
3 crashed out   6 walk ... through

B Word order

Refer students to the section on phrasal verbs on page R40–1 in the dictionary and make sure they have read it before doing the following exercises.

13.2 Write the following on the board:

If you don't understand the word, look up in your dictionary.
Who looked after when you were sick?

Elicit the fact that the sentences are incorrect without an object. Ask them to put *it* into the first sentence and *you* into the second. Where should the object go in each case? Refer students to the phrasal verb section of the verb **look**. The symbol ↔ in the phrasal verb **look up** shows that the two parts of the verb can be separated by the object, while **look after** is inseparable, so the sentences above should read *look it up* and *looked after you*.

Give students some time alone to complete the exercise, and then ask them to check their answers in pairs before class feedback.

KEY
1 copy me in
2 checked into the hotel
3 phone in my order/phone my order in

4 pass by the post office
5 turned off the light that had been shining in her eyes
6 chop down that old oak tree/chop that old oak tree down
7 singled him out
8 missed out an *m* in *accommodation*

C Travel and computers

13.3 Divide students into groups of four and ask each student to look up one column of phrasal verbs only. They should check the meaning of their verbs in the dictionary alone. Then in their groups of four they should tell each other what their verbs mean. They can then put the verbs into the correct column.

During class feedback, you could get students to give you a sentence using each phrasal verb.

KEY

computers	travel
drill down	check into sth
fall over	take off
scan sth in	touch down
back sth up	stop over
jack into sth	get away
log off	set off

D The meaning of particles

Explain that there is usually a meaning associated with the particles, which should help students to remember phrasal verbs. One particle may have several different meanings.

13.4 Tell students that the particle **up** can be used in many different ways, including its literal meaning referring to movement to a higher position, the meaning of 'increasing', or to give an idea of improving something. They should use their dictionaries to help them with this exercise.

KEY **movement**: dig, hoover
increase: ratchet, step
improve: juice, spruce

14 Synonyms and opposites

A Synonyms

Write the word **angry** on the board and ask students to give you other words with a similar meaning, for example **annoyed**, **irritated**, **furious**, etc. Explain to students that in many of the entries in the dictionary there is information on *synonyms*, or words with similar meanings. This is sometimes indicated within an entry by the symbol **SYN**, followed by a word with a similar meaning to the headword, for example after the definition for **annoy**, the word **irritate** is given. Sometimes there is a longer note at the end of an entry, which deals with several words with similar meaning and explains the similarities and differences between them, for example at the entry for **angry**.

14.1 To make this exercise more interesting, you could write the words on separate pieces of paper and give one to each student in the class. They should check the meaning of their word in the dictionary if necessary, and then move around the class trying to find their partner, i.e. the student who has a word that is close in meaning to their own.

Check answers as a class to see if students have paired up correctly.

KEY

preposterous	outrageous
egocentric	selfish
dramatist	playwright
synthetic	man-made
singly	individually
fortunately	luckily
demoralize	dishearten
jut	project

14.2 Refer students to the entry for **cheap**. They should use the information in the note to complete the exercise. Get students to check their answers in pairs before going through the answers as a class, using the information in brackets to help students understand why each answer is correct.

KEY
1 cheap (*used in a disapproving way*)
2 reasonable (*used particularly of prices*)
3 competitive (*competitive is a positive word, which is suitable for this context*)
4 budget (*fits the advertising context*)
5 inexpensive (*budget is only really used in advertising and does not fit the context here.*)

14.3 Refer students to the note at the entry for **trip** for this exercise. Again, pairwork would be useful before class feedback.

KEY
1 tour (*includes visits to several places*)
2 excursions (*short trips made for pleasure*)
3 expedition (*a journey with a particular purpose*)
4 journey (*long and difficult*)
5 trip (*collocates with business*)

14.4 Refer students to the note at the entry for **think** for this exercise. Again, pairwork would be useful before class feedback.

KEY
1 believe (*used for matters of principle*)
2 reckon (*used when you think that sth is possible*)
3 feel (*used for an opinion about what you should do*)
4 was under the impression (*used when you have an idea that sth is true*)
5 think (*used for matters of taste*)

14.5 The answers to all these questions are to be found in the 'A OR B?' sections within the *Synonyms* notes. Do the first question together as a class to make sure that students know where to look for the answers.

KEY
1 ... *a terrible fear*... (**fright** *cannot be used for things that always frighten you*)
2 correct (**simple** *collocates with* **reason**)
3 *The court declared...* (**declare** *is used for giving judgements*)
4 correct (*used when a direct connection is made between cause and effect*)
5 ... *strongly advise...* (*used to warn about possible dangers*)
6 ... *minor illnesses...* (**disease** *is always severe*)
7 correct (*used when you are looking for mistakes*)
8 ... *inaccurate map* (*something that contains incorrect facts is* **inaccurate**)
9 correct (*used when talking about particular cases*)
10 ... *refused to comment* (**refuse** *is not used in this way with* **remark**)

14.6 This exercise is designed to encourage students to broaden their active vocabulary by using slightly less frequent, but more precise and appropriate words. Do the first question as a class to ensure that students understand what they have to do. They will need plenty of time to complete the exercise, but they should check their ideas in small groups before you go through the answers as a class. As you do so, get students to tell you why each answer is appropriate.

KEY
1 protest (*especially publicly*)
2 intimidate (*to frighten or threaten sb so that they will do what you want*)
3 aching (*used for a continuous dull pain*)
4 elderly (*a more polite word than* **old**)
5 produce (*things connected with farming*)
6 tow (*used for pulling a vehicle*)
7 motive (*explains someone's behaviour, especially their reason for committing a crime*)
8 chores (*boring and unpleasant tasks*)
9 get (*used particularly about jokes*)
10 witty (*trying to be clever*)

B Opposites

After the symbol **OPP** students will find words with a meaning which is the opposite of the headword, for example at the entry for **nervous**.

14.7 When checking answers as a class, give students or elicit from them the information in brackets below.

KEY 1 immature, immortal, implausible, impractical, *irrelevant* (im– only precedes adjectives and adverbs beginning with *m* or *p*)

2 disadvantage, disagree, disapprove, *uncomfortable*, discontented

3 unconvincing, unfortunately, unintentional, *illogical*, unmanageable

4 incompetent, inefficient, inexcusable, *non-flammable*, insincere (**inflammable** is a word, but it means the same as **flammable**)

5 non-alcoholic, non-fiction, *unremarkable*, non-renewable, non-returnable

14.8 This exercise will reinforce the use of prefixes demonstrated in the previous exercise.

KEY
1 disagree
2 non-renewable
3 inexcusable
4 unconvincing (*or* illogical)
5 inefficient (*or* impractical)

14.9 These last two exercises will further raise students' awareness of prefixes. They can both be attempted without looking at the dictionary, before checking ideas in the dictionary.

KEY logical, relevant, efficient, flammable

14.10
KEY dis–

15 Collocations

A What are collocations?

Write the following on the board:

Merry   Christmas
Happy   Birthday

Ask students if you can switch the words **merry** and **happy** in these phrases. Demonstrate that while you can say *Happy Christmas*, you can't say *Merry Birthday*, even though there is little difference between the words *merry* and *happy*. These are examples of collocations, or 'words that go together'. While **happy** collocates with both **Christmas** and **Birthday**, **merry** only collocates with **Christmas**.

For more information on collocations, students should look at page R48 in the dictionary.

15.1 Refer students to the entries for **chance**, **hope** and **word**. Point out that common collocations are highlighted in bold in the examples in these entries. The following three exercises focus on this feature of the dictionary.

KEY 1 'a small chance'
2 *a slight chance/an outside chance*
3 *no chance; a slim chance; a fifty-fifty chance; a very good chance*

15.2
KEY 1 *raise your hopes/get your hopes up*
2 *have high hopes of…*
3 *give up hope*
4 *live in hope*
5 *a glimmer of hope*

15.3 Give students some time alone to look at these collocations in context. Then put them into pairs to talk about what the phrases mean before checking answers as a class.

KEY 1 from your own understanding, not just repeating what other people have said
2 in every possible way
3 manage to express
4 does not express it strongly enough

B Adverbs

15.4 Allocate one word to each student in the class. Give them a minute or two to check meaning, pronunciation, etc. of their word in the dictionary. Students should then move around the class trying to find someone who has a word that collocates with their own. Go through answers as a class, making sure that students have paired up correctly.

KEY
bitterly cold
flatly refuse
highly productive
immensely powerful
narrowly miss
painfully slow
strictly confidential
strongly advise

C Adjective + noun

In the first exercise, students are looking for a word that intensifies the noun, one that means something similar to 'big' with each set of words. Again, they should look at the examples section of the noun entries to find suitable adjectives. They could work in pairs to complete the exercise, so that they don't all have to look up all the words. The second exercise, using some of these pairs, can be done individually.

15.5
KEY **heavy** rain/traffic/heart/defeat/smoker
strong wind/smell/views/language/probability
high cost/heel/summer/hopes/society
sharp frost/drop/wit/relief/contrast
broad accent/grin/hint/spread/generalization

15.6
KEY 1 Heavy traffic
2 strong language
3 high hopes
4 sharp frost
5 broad… accent

D Verb + noun

15.7 At class feedback, write five columns on the board with the headings *do*, *make*, *have*, *give* and *take*. As you go through the answers, write the nouns under the correct heading. Point out to students that this a good way of recording vocabulary information.

KEY
1 do
2 have
3 give
4 make (*British English*), take
5 made
6 gave
7 make
8 take
9 giving
10 do

15.8 Students can try this alone without their dictionary to begin with.

KEY 1 *hung his head*
2 correct
3 correct
4 *wipe your feet*
5 correct
6 *shrugging her shoulders*
7 *sprained my ankle*
8 correct

E Phrases

15.9 You could do this exercise in a similar way to the adverb + adjective exercise 15.4. You should also focus students on the pronunciation of **and** in each phrase, i.e. /ən/, and get students to say the phrases in a natural way. The second exercise will ensure that students understand the meaning of the phrases. Get students to check their answers in pairs before going through the answers as a class.

KEY
aims and objectives
bribery and corruption
bright and cheerful
hustle and bustle
long and hard
push and shove
really and truly
rules and regulations
scrimp and save

15.10

KEY
1	bribery and corruption	6	rules and regulations
2	scrimped and saved	7	pushing and shoving
3	hustle and bustle	8	bright and cheerful
4	long and hard	9	really and truly
5	aims and objectives		

16 Compounds

A Compound nouns

There is often no fixed rule about whether a compound is written as two words, with a hyphen, or joined together as one word. Compounds which are so common that they are fixed tend to be written as one word (e.g. **teacup**; compare **coffee cup**); ones where the relationship between the elements is looser tend to be written separately (e.g. **traffic light**). Where the compound is derived from a phrase (e.g. **double-decker**: a bus which has a double deck), the word tends to be hyphenated.

16.1 Encourage students to search for the compounds in the proximity of the main entry. All of these words have their own separate entry, but sometimes compounds (where the relationship between the elements is less fixed) can also be found in examples (e.g. **instant coffee**).

KEY
1	teacup	4	five-a-side	7	double glazing
2	coffee machine	5	double-decker	8	sea fish
3	seabird	6	sleeping bag		

16.2 Students should attempt this exercise without their dictionaries, then check their answers using them. During feedback, discuss the meanings of the compounds. **Drama queen**, **stuffed shirt**, **asylum seeker** and **paper tiger** can refer to people.

KEY
soap opera	stuffed shirt
drama queen	asylum seeker
ski jump	paper tiger
sniffer dog	

16.3 This exercise gives practice in explaining the relationship between elements in compounds. Encourage students to use the structure *is used for…* followed by the *–ing* form.

KEY
1 A bottle opener is used for opening bottles.
2 An answering machine is used for answering phone calls and recording messages.
3 A shoehorn is used for putting on shoes.
4 A clothes horse is used for drying clothes.
5 A petrol pump/gas pump is used for filling cars with petrol/gas.
6 A paper clip is used for holding loose pieces of paper together.

16.4 This exercise looks at words that refer to people who do particular jobs. Some make use of the suffix *–er*, others *–man* or *–woman*. This second type is becoming less common as it is considered to be sexist to make reference to a person's sex when this has no bearing on their work. As a result, forms like **firefighter** are considered more acceptable than **fireman** and **firewoman**.

KEY
1	a piano tuner	3	a firefighter	5	a window cleaner
2	a fisherman	4	a glass-blower		

B Compound adjectives

These compounds, formed from an adjective, adverb or noun plus a past participle, are all used to talk about particular attributes of a person.

16.5
KEY
1	soft-hearted	4	eagle-eyed
2	sharp-tongued	5	fair-haired
3	open-minded	6	softly-spoken

17 Register in language

OALD gives information about the appropriacy of a word in particular situations: whether, for example, it is mainly used in informal language such as conversations with friends or letters to friends and family, or formal language, literary style, or academic writing. In other words, it gives you information about the *register* of a word.

A Register labels

17.1 Students should work in pairs to research the meanings of these register labels.

17.2 To ensure that students also focus on the meaning of these expressions, discuss possible situations in which these expressions might be used.

KEY
grizzled	literary
culture vulture	humorous
big deal!	ironic, informal
execrable	formal
get a load of sth	informal
recce	informal
yo	slang
alluvial	technical

B Formal and informal

Small and **good** are adjectives that can be used in almost any situation. They have no special label in the dictionary. The words in these exercises are more restricted in their use. Students should work on the exercises in pairs, using their dictionaries to check any words as they go.

17.3
KEY
tiddly	less formal
diminutive	more formal
teensy-weensy	less formal
titchy	less formal
infinitesimal	more formal
wee	less formal

17.4
KEY *In order of formality:* gnarly, mega, brill, neat, ace, cracking, excellent, outstanding, wondrous, sublime

17.5
KEY
1	no	2	no	3	yes	4	no

C Informal alternatives

17.6 The words in these exercises are routinely substituted for their more formal equivalents, especially in the spoken language. In some cases the informal variant is more common than the word it replaces. In the first exercise, students should use their dictionaries to find any words they are not familiar with; in the second they should guess before checking in their dictionaries.

KEY
1 maths (math *in North American English*)
2 admin (*British English*)
3 chimps, hippos and rhinos
4 op (*British English*)
5 info
6 shades

17.7
KEY
pins	legs	ticker	heart
tootsies	toes	mitts	hands
choppers	teeth	shell-like	ear

D Attitude

By choosing a particular word, people often show what their attitude is to the person or thing that they are talking or writing about. Some words tend to be used when the speaker or writer feels positive towards somebody or something. These words are labelled *approving* in the dictionary. Other words show that the person talking or writing has a more critical attitude. These are labelled *disapproving*. Students should tackle these exercises on their own before using the dictionary to check their answers.

17.8
KEY

1	positive	5	critical	9	positive
2	critical	6	positive	10	critical
3	positive	7	critical		
4	critical	8	positive		

E Good or bad?

17.9
KEY

1	positive	3	critical	5	positive	7	positive
2	positive	4	positive	6	positive	8	positive

18 English around the world

A Varieties of English

OALD gives information about the different words that are used in varieties of English around the world, not only in British and American English. These exercises are designed to raise awareness of these varieties and to familiarize students with the labels used in the dictionary.

In these exercises students should try to identify the labels, words or sentences individually, then check their own work in the dictionary. Note that the label *US* is used for words which are used only in the US, and *NAmE* for words used in North America, including Canada.

18.1
KEY

NAmE	North American English
US	US English
BrE	British English
ScotE	Scottish English
IrishE	Irish English
AustralE	Australian English
SAfrE	South African English
SEAsianE	South-East Asian English
NZE	New Zealand English
IndE	Indian English
NEngE	the English of northern England

18.2
KEY

outwith	Scotland
checkers	North America
cobber	Australia and New Zealand
lakh	India
frogmarch	Britain
beltway	the US

18.3
KEY

1	South Africa	5	Australia	9	East Africa
2	Africa	6	Canada	10	New Zealand
3	India	7	Wales	11	Scotland
4	Ireland	8	South-East Asia		

B British and American English

18.4 In American English and British English there are many words which have the same meaning and use but are spelled differently. See if students already know any of these differences. This exercise draws attention to some systematic differences.

KEY

American spelling	British spelling
center	centre
humor	humour
analog	analogue
esthetic	aesthetic
analyze	analyse
mustache	moustache
plow	plough
armor	armour

defense	defence
maneuver	manoeuvre
medalist	medallist
instill	instil

18.5 There are also special notes about some words whose meanings differ in American English and British English. There is a list of these notes on page R94 of the dictionary.

KEY

1	true	3	false	5	false
2	true	4	false		

18.6 Some words are used in both British English and American English, but they are more common in one variety than the other. **Tailpipe**, for example, is labelled *especially AmE*, which means that it is common in American English but less widely used in British English. Students should discuss these words in pairs.

KEY They are all used especially in British or American English.

C British and American pronunciation

The dictionary also shows you when a word, or part of a word, is pronounced differently in British and American English. These exercises draw attention to the different possible pronunciations of *o* and other sounds in British and North American English, and differences in stress. Students should work in pairs before feeding back to the class.

18.7
KEY **hot**: /hɒt/ in British English, /hɑːt/ in American English
dog: /dɒg/ in British English, /dɔːg/ in American English
boat: /bəʊt/ in British English, /boʊt/ in American English
bought: /bɔːt/ in British English and American English

18.8
KEY

1	optimist	3	sallow	5	fastener	7	astute
2	dogma	4	voluntary	6	paternal		

18.9
KEY

in British English	in North American English
<u>glac</u>é	glac<u>é</u>
<u>lab</u>oratory	lab<u>o</u>ratory
<u>perfum</u>	perf<u>ume</u>
<u>dec</u>or	dec<u>or</u>

D Words from other languages

18.10 A large proportion of the vocabulary of English has come from other sources. This exercise is designed to show the variety of these sources. Students should be encouraged to pay attention to the meaning when doing the exercise, and their findings can be discussed during feedback.

KEY

machismo	Spanish	meze	Turkish
gesundheit	German	ergo	Latin
crescendo	Italian	soupçon	French
haiku	Japanese	favela	Portuguese
wok	Chinese	babushka	Russian

E Dishes of the world quiz

18.11 This exercise can be done in teams as a competition.

KEY

moussaka	Greece	mealies	South Africa
nachos	Mexico	couscous	North Africa
tempura	Japan	vindaloo	India
haggis	Scotland	grits	the US
balti	Pakistan	cassoulet	France

19 The Oxford 3000™

The *Oxford 3000* is a list of the most important 3000 words in English. They include the words used most frequently, the words used across a variety of types of English, and the words which teachers consider to be the most important for their students to know. The list, with a full introduction, can be found on page R99 of the dictionary; it can also be downloaded from the *OALD* website (www.oup.com/elt/oald).

You will also see that the words which make up the *Oxford 3000* are printed in larger type in the main A – Z section of the dictionary, and are followed by a key symbol ☞ . These keyword entries give extra help and information about how the word is used. Many of the keywords have several meanings and are used in a variety of phrases, idioms, etc.

OALD not only allows students to find meanings and spellings of words, it also shows them how words are related and enables them to explore further. These exercises show students some ways in which they can use the features of the dictionary to broaden their vocabulary.

A Keywords

19.1 This exercise is designed to introduce students to the *Oxford 3000*. They should look at the dictionary extract and read the questions. The answers can be discussed as a class. Make sure that by the end students are aware of the fact that keywords are the most important words to learn, and know how to recognize them.

KEY
1 **Website** and **wedding** are printed in larger type and are followed by a key symbol.
2 Because they occur more frequently and are more important for learners.
3 **Wed** is old-fashioned, or used only in newspapers. **Wedded** is formal.
4 12 compounds with **wedding** are mentioned.

B Find a word

19.2 Show students the *Oxford 3000* list on page R100 of their dictionaries. Explain that this lists contains all the keywords marked with a key in the main A – Z section of the dictionary. More advanced students will be interested to read the introduction. The words needed to fill in the blanks in this exercise are all *Oxford 3000* words.

KEY
1 hard
2 point
3 space
4 height
5 spell
6 squeeze

C High-frequency words

It is important to know high-frequency words well. Students may think that they already know all there is to know about these words, but these exercises will show that there is more to a word than its basic meaning. **Say** is the 34th most frequent word in the corpus, and **time** is the 56th.

Both exercises can be done as a competition between groups of around four or five students. The winners will be the group who find most answers in the allocated time. Allow 10 or 15 minutes for each exercise and then discuss the answers as a class.

19.3
KEY
1 verb, exclamation
2 informal, US
3 'Hello!' I said
4 no
5 again
6 no
7 She told me the news
8 Britain

19.4
KEY
1 verb
2 *badly*
3 *what time do you make it?*
4 *in time*
5 *in ancient times*
6 *behind the times*
7 *lose*
8 *I have been to London*

D Vocabulary building

19.5 Special *Vocabulary building* notes gather together words with related meanings. You can find a list of these on page R93.

Tell students to look at the *Vocabulary building* note at the entry for **laugh** and read through the different expressions. All the words mean 'laugh', but each denotes a particular way of laughing. Students should then replace the verb in these sentences with one of the verbs in the box.

KEY
1 chuckled
2 snigger
3 cackled
4 giggled
5 roared

E Word families

19.6 When learning a word, it is useful to get to know the other members of its family (its derivatives). As an example, show students the entry for **explain**. In the Word family box they will find information about the noun that is related to **explain** (**explanation**), and two related adjectives, **explanatory** and **explicable** (with its opposite **inexplicable**).

KEY

noun	verb	adjective
truth	——	true
reliability/reliance	rely	reliable
stability	stabilize	stable
ally	ally	allied
accusation	accuse	accusing/accusatory
division	divide	divisive

F Prefixes and suffixes

19.7 The *Oxford 3000* contains a number of prefixes and suffixes which can be used to form new words, including words which are not in the dictionary because they are created *ad hoc*. Tell students to look at the entries for the prefixes and suffixes in the box, then try the exercise.

Compounds formed with these prefixes and suffixes sometimes have a have a hyphen and sometimes do not. *Re–* and *–ish* are generally used without a hyphen. In British English a hyphen is generally used for the others, especially when these words are new formations and not given in the dictionary. In American English the hyphen is not generally used with *non–*, but is used with the others.

KEY
1 mid-
2 non-
3 anti-
4 ex-
5 re-
6 -ish
7 self-
8 -sized

G Language study terms

19.8 Students should look at the list of language study terms on page R113 of the dictionary before doing this exercise. Knowing these words will help them to use the dictionary more effectively.

KEY

parts of speech	punctuation marks	parts of a word	register
determiner	comma	syllable	slang
preposition	semicolon	suffix	dialect
pronoun	apostrophe	prefix	ironic

20 Arts words

Although the *Oxford 3000* list makes an excellent starting point for vocabulary study, students will certainly need to learn other words apart from these. You will find a specialist list for those whose area of work or study is the arts and humanities on page R114 of the dictionary. These words are the next most important words to learn after the *Oxford 3000* for those who are interested in literature, painting, music, etc. The list is based on analyses of specialist corpora and includes the next most frequent words in arts and humanities texts after the keywords of the *Oxford 3000*. Knowing them will help students to understand texts about these subjects more easily.

A People in the arts

20.1 The answers to this exercise all refer to people who are involved in the arts.

KEY
1 critic
2 novelist
3 collector
4 composer
5 conductor
6 architect
7 curator
8 dealer
9 choreographer
10 poet
11 publisher
12 sculptor

B Prepositions

20.2 Students should do this exercise individually, then check their answers in the dictionary.

KEY
1 to	3 of	5 into	7 to
2 with	4 from	6 by	

C Stress

20.3 Words that are similar to each other in spelling are often pronounced in different ways. Once students have completed the exercise, see if they can draw any general rules for the shift in stress. (The suffixes *–graphy*, *–grapher*, *–ural* send the stress to the syllable immediately before, whereas the suffixes *–graphic*, *–ition* and *–ation* are stressed.).

KEY
arch<u>i</u>tect	archi<u>tec</u>ture	archi<u>tec</u>tural
chore<u>o</u>graphy	chore<u>og</u>rapher	choreo<u>graph</u>ic
com<u>pose</u>	com<u>pos</u>er	compo<u>si</u>tion
<u>narr</u>ative	nar<u>ra</u>tor	nar<u>ra</u>tion
or<u>ches</u>tra	or<u>ches</u>tral	orches<u>tra</u>tion
<u>poet</u>	<u>poet</u>ry	po<u>et</u>ic

D Art forms

20.4 This exercise, and others like it, will help students to build up a mental map of the vocabulary of the arts.

KEY
literature	performing arts	visual arts
sonnet	ballet	watercolour
prose	opera	portrait
biography	symphony	canvas
fiction	solo	abstract
narrator	quartet	installation

21 Science words

You will find a specialist list for those whose area of work or study is science and technology on page R115 of the dictionary. These words are the next most important words to learn after the *Oxford 3000* for those who are interested in physics, chemistry, biology, etc. The list is based on analyses of specialist corpora and includes the next most frequent words in scientific texts after the keywords of the *Oxford 3000*. Knowing them will help students to understand texts about these subjects more easily.

A Scientific and technical fields

21.1 This exercise presents words which refer to various scientific and technical disciplines. Point out that the *–ics* ending, despite appearances, is singular, as in **mathematics**.

KEY
1 agriculture	3 conservation	5 genetics	7 statistics
2 cloning	4 computing	6 geology	

21.2 This exercise will help students to build up a mental map of the vocabulary of the sciences.

KEY
biology	physics	astronomy	mathematics
embryo	electron	galaxy	axis
mammal	ion	orbit	binary
mutation	laser	satellite	equation
organism	radiation	solar	fraction

B Chemical elements

21.3 Once students have completed the table they can report their findings to the class. For example: *Copper is an element with the scientific symbol Cu. It is used for making electric wires, pipes and coins.*

KEY
name of element	scientific symbol	information
copper	Cu	used for making electric wires, pipes and coins
carbon	C	found in all living things, diamonds
oxygen	O	present in air and water
calcium	Ca	found in bones, teeth and chalk
sodium	Na	found in compounds such as salt
hydrogen	H	the lightest element; present in water

C Talking about scientific results

21.4 This exercise introduces some general vocabulary used in all branches of science, in particular when talking about the results of experiments, research, etc.

KEY
1 widespread	3 isolated	5 random	7 long-term
2 scattered	4 findings	6 phenomena	

22 Business and finance words

You will find a specialist list for those whose area of work or study is business and finance on page R116 of the dictionary. These words are the next most important words to learn after the *Oxford 3000* for those who are interested in these subjects. The list is based on analyses of specialist corpora and includes the next most frequent words in business and finance texts after the keywords of the *Oxford 3000*. Knowing them will help students to understand texts about these subjects more easily.

A People in the world of business

22.1 The answers to this exercise all refer to people who are involved in the world of business.

KEY
1 accountant	4 banker	7 economist	10 trader
2 analyst	5 broker	8 operator	
3 auditor	6 contractor	9 retailer	

B Related words

22.2 The words in these pairs have related meanings, and are often found in close proximity to each other.

KEY
asset	liability	gross	net/nett
boom	recession	lender	borrower
creditor	debtor	purchaser	seller
landlord	tenant	surplus	deficit

C Prepositions

22.3 Students should do this exercise individually, then check their answers in the dictionary.

KEY
1 on	3 with	5 to	7 for
2 to	4 to	6 on	8 for

D Word combinations

22.4 This exercise focuses on words which are collocates of items on the Business and finance list.

KEY
1 jobs	2 profits	3 policy	4 small

23 New words

New words are entering English all the time, whether from new technology, new fashions, or things in the news. Although these new words form a small proportion of the vocabulary of English, they often receive a lot of attention in the media, and people find them interesting or amusing – or sometimes vulgar or ephemeral. Like the things they refer to, however, it is difficult to imagine the modern world without them. These exercises focus on recent arrivals which students may be interested in. They can all be tackled individually, with students then comparing ideas in pairs, then feeding back to the whole class.